TWO BRAINS
ONE AIM

Also by Eric Smiley

Look...No Hands!

TWO BRAINS
ONE AIM

A Riding Coach's
Key Concepts for Bringing
Horse and Rider Together
(and Ending in Success!)

ERIC SMILEY, FBHS

with Ellie Hughes

TRAFALGAR SQUARE
North Pomfret, Vermont

First published in 2019 by
Trafalgar Square Books
North Pomfret, Vermont 05053

Disclaimer of Liability
The author and publisher shall have neither liability nor responsibility to any person or entity with respect to any loss or damage caused or alleged to be caused directly or indirectly by the information contained in this book. While the book is as accurate as the author can make it, there may be errors, omissions, and inaccuracies.

Trafalgar Square Books encourages the use of approved safety helmets in all equestrian sports and activities.

Library of Congress Cataloging-in-Publication Data
Names: Smiley, Eric, 1951- author. | Hughes, Ellie, author.
Title: Two brains, one aim : a riding coach's key concepts for bringing horse and rider together (and ending in success!) / Eric Smiley with Ellie Hughes.
Description: North Pomfret, Vermont : Trafalgar Square Books, 2019. | Includes index. | Includes index.
Identifiers: LCCN 2018037116 (print) | LCCN 2018052957 (ebook) | ISBN 9781570769412 | ISBN 9781570768927
Subjects: LCSH: Horsemanship. | Horses--Training.
Classification: LCC SF309 (ebook) | LCC SF309 .S623 2019 (print) | DDC 798.2--dc23
LC record available at https://lccn.loc.gov/2018037116

All photographs by Orla Murphy-LaScola except Michel Chretinat p. 145 top; Fiona Scott-Maxwell pp. 37, 149, 153, 161 right & bottom; Irina Kuzmina p. iv, 147 bottom, 148, 177; Maria Sage 34, 36, 41; Michele Flanders p. 146; Tyree of Smugmug! p. 145 bottom.

Book design by Lauryl Eddlemon
Cover design by RM Didier
Index by Andrea Jones (JonesLiteraryServices.com)
Typefaces: Proxima Nova, Chaparral Pro

Printed in China
10 9 8 7 6 5 4 3 2 1

To Sue, my soulmate and wife,
who continues to make my
journey with riding and coaching,
and our life together with horses,
an absolute delight.

CONTENTS

CHAPTER ONE

Introduction

My school reports always used to read, "Eric finds academia difficult and seems to enjoy sport more. I expect he will develop later in life." How true that proved to be. It wasn't that I was stupid—I scored highly in IQ tests—but I couldn't figure out **how** to learn. I struggled to break down information into understandable chunks that I could store and readily retrieve.

I started to find answers in the army, to which I was dispatched shortly after leaving school. I joined the 5th Royal Inniskilling Dragoon Guards, a Cavalry regiment with a strong equestrian heritage. During a six-week course at the Royal Army Veterinary Corps at Melton Mowbray in Leicestershire, England, I met Captain Ben Jones, the chief instructor there at the time. Captain Jones was once a prominent member of the British Eventing team, and he demonstrated the hows and whys I had missed in my earlier riding.

> In our quest for progress, we are often guilty of dressing up simple instructions in complicated language.

With its structured, orderly regime and clearly defined boundaries, the army forced me to think about things in a similar way. I discovered that when I used this process to break down information, I could reassemble it and deliver instructions clearly and concisely. Once I had figured this out, life became easier, not only as a rider, but also as a coach. I believe there are many people like me—people in need of a method of learning that allows them to realize their potential.

My life is spent watching horses and riders and how they interact. I try to understand what is happening and why. Equestrian sport has evolved enormously in recent years, and in our quest for progress, we are often guilty of dressing up simple instructions in complicated language. When coaches, trainers, instructors, and clinicians fall into this trap, it makes understanding difficult and slows down a rider's natural responses.

I try to use words that make sense to me. When a coach cannot deliver a simple instruction clearly, how is a rider expected to relay it to the horse?

This is one of the reasons I wanted to write this book: to demystify some of the most common misconceptions that stand in the way of progress.

Olympic gold-medal-winning cyclist Sir Bradley Wiggins once said, "Don't look too far ahead or you will lose sight of what is in front of you." This applies in every walk of life.

I hope this book will enlighten and inform those who seek to enjoy and make progress in their riding. By keeping explanations and illustrations simple I don't mean to sound patronizing; I am merely doing what all top sports people do—focusing on what is important.

Who Should Read the Pages That Follow

This book is aimed at riders, coaches, and anyone interested in learning more about how humans and horses interact. I have tried to harness my own experiences when I cover the three main disciplines—dressage, show jumping, and eventing—and how they relate to one another. I look at how those in a coaching position can guide riders to perform better by making their lives less complicated and more fulfilling, and I examine how riders can apply the same principles to training their horses and become self-sufficient.

It is important to understand how we learn, how horses learn, and how information is imparted, retained, and retrieved in a useful way. I voice my likes and dislikes, my dos and don'ts, and my preferred ways—with reasons. At times, I may appear destructive, but I always try to rebuild in a logical and positive way.

Welcome to My World

Throughout my riding career—from the very earliest days to the present—I have had limited help. There are many reasons for this, but in no way do I feel that I have missed out. The help I have received, for the most part, has been a stimulus for me to improve what I was already doing or to find a different way that would help me achieve my goals.

You'll find that throughout this book I talk about the "coach," but not everyone has an actual person fulfilling this role. I intend the word "coach" to be all-encompassing, applying to whomever or whatever in your life provides guidance and advises. This might be a regular instructor, an occasional teacher, a clinician, a team coach, or a knowledgeable and experienced friend. Equally, it might be an expert via a book or video, or an article in a magazine.

You should be open to all forms of input—not least from the horse himself—and be able to understand where each snippet fits into the process of learning. Whatever the source, it must stimulate a curiosity, a questioning of what is said or written. This should not be in a doubting or disbelieving way, but in a way that ensures clarity and understanding.

> You should be open to all forms of input—not least from the horse himself.

The aim of this book is twofold. Firstly, to improve the relationship between coach (in all its guises) and rider and horse; in other words, help the rider learn how to learn, as well as guide those who help others in an instructional capacity make the way they communicate clearer. Secondly, to give those who do not have regular tutelage techniques and practical exercises to help develop riding and training skills.

It is important to remember that being taught is only part of the process of learning. Good horsemanship—something that should be at the forefront of everybody's mind—is the art of understanding the horse, his welfare, and how you interact and care for him.

My specialist discipline is eventing: a combined sport of dressage, cross-country, and show jumping. It has therefore been a requirement for me to be proficient in the training and execution of all three of these. When my international career as a rider started to wind down and I made the transition to coaching, the training and experience I'd had in all three disciplines allowed me to understand the process that others needed to go through in their journey of learning. The lessons I've learned and would like to share are therefore applicable across all disciplines.

How It Works

This book is not meant to be an instructional tome. It is designed to cover the subjects I feel are relevant to help people learn how to process information, understand their horses, and be more self-sufficient in their journey toward becoming horsemen and horsewomen.

With this in mind I have covered the subjects that follow in a logical way. To begin with, you should know how you learn. You should understand the methods of communicating, retaining, and using information. Some of the common problems related to these areas are also helpful to know.

It is also important to comprehend how the animal you are working with learns and uses information. A much over-used statement in the horse world is "build a solid foundation." What does this mean in the journey you are undertaking with your horse? I explain what it means to the rider, the horse, and the source of any help you might get. Those supporting the rider and horse have a huge role in the end result.

The journey of becoming better horsemen and horsewomen has common ground within *all* disciplines. This common ground is explained by demonstrating exercises that work for us all. When you decide where you have a preferred interest, you might choose to compete in order to measure your training accomplishments, so I also take you along the competition road of how to achieve "the best you can." There are many ways this can be achieved, but one thing is for certain: having a route map is better than trusting to luck.

Enjoy the journey.

1.1 At the start of every day I look at this picture and smile. There is no doubt of the outcome. But oh, how everyone is enjoying the journey.

CHAPTER TWO

How You Learn

DNA is the unique genetic fingerprint that makes us who we are. From its use in solving murders to its importance in parent testing in humans and animals, it represents a giant leap forward in science. The way DNA has shaped history fascinates me.

If "you are who you are" and certain things cannot be changed due to your DNA, does that also mean "you do what you do" and that every outcome is predictable?

In certain people, yes.

As a coach, my job is to guide and educate. Do I make a lasting difference? This is a question I expect all teachers ask at the end of a tiring day! Sometimes the answer is unclear; sometimes it is obvious. Often, I watch my pupils compete and wonder whether I am seeing tangible evidence of anything I have taught them or whether I am merely witnessing what would have happened anyway. This is not me doubting myself; it is me trying to be objective so that I can refine what I do.

I am fascinated by what and how much information the human and equine brains are able to retain. But there is a big difference between the two: one is evolving rapidly in today's high-tech society, while the other has changed very little in thousands of years.

How is harmony to develop between horse and rider when one has aims and ambitions and the other is happy eating grass? Is it possible to

How is harmony to develop between horse and rider when one has aims and ambitions and the other is happy eating grass?

predetermine how both will do on their educational journey?

When teaching I am confronted with many questions, choices, and possibilities. Sometimes there are constraints that are outside my control, sometimes I have to prioritize and decide what it is possible to achieve within a given timeframe. Often, I might need to change direction and alter my priorities in response to a situation that arises.

My ultimate goal is to harmonize a partnership and to give clarity to horse and rider. Both parties need to enjoy the journey and the experience, and for this reason, a clear route map is essential.

Methods of Learning

Information can both enhance and detract from performance. Much depends upon how and when it is delivered, and how well it is learned and retrieved. The information needs to be relevant and appropriate for the recipient's level and stage of training and because no two individuals are the same, it needs to be tailored to suit.

Nature or Nurture?

I once attended a science fair at which young people were taught the principles of science in the workplace. There were various experiments on display, all designed to engage, enthuse, and challenge the youngsters. It was fascinating to watch them experiment and then try some of the puzzles myself. It soon became apparent that games, which seemed easy to some, proved challenging to others, and vice versa. This is not a new concept. We all have different strengths and weaknesses—it is why we end up in different professions—but it begs some very important questions:

➤ Is it possible to override some of the things we are not so good at?

➤ If there is a desire and a method readily available, can we change what is imprinted in our being?

➤ At what stage does nature click back in again and make us revert to the imprinted version of ourselves?

To be able to input, retain, and retrieve information and skills, we need a method. The following are mental techniques that I have found very useful, both in my career as a competitive rider and, latterly, as a communicator.

1 The Jigsaw Method

Children are often given jigsaw puzzles to solve. At first they are easy, then as children understand the method and logic, puzzles become more challenging.

Figure 2.1 is a picture of German Olympian Michael Jung's two-time Olympic champion La Biosthetique Sam FBW, arguably one of the greatest event horses of all time. Let us say Sam has five qualities that make him so successful: rideability, a good mind, bravery, carefulness, and soundness. Let us put these attributes into a five-piece jigsaw. Each piece has one of these words or phrases on it (fig. 2.1).

You can then make the five-piece jigsaw into a 15- or 25-piece jigsaw by taking each quality and subdividing it into a further three to five qualities:

2.1 **Every piece of the jigsaw puzzle is made up of a quality that develops as a partnership grows, which makes it a useful learning technique.**

> ➤ Rideability: regular gaits, forward thinking, straight, adjustable, balanced.

> ➤ Good mind: understands the training, confident in the rider, at peace with himself, accepting of crowds, comfortable in his surroundings.

➤ Brave: has been given a good start, no hang-ups, always given a good ride, knows what partnership means, jumping ability.

➤ Careful: natural care, has a conscience, is rideable, has scope, has a good canter.

➤ Sound: good conformation, well shod, well managed, fit, good veterinary care.

This is easy to understand because the progression from the initial puzzle is logical and relevant to the subject. The size of the puzzle—whether it has 5, 15, 25, or 50 pieces—will depend on the stage of training of both horse and rider, the time available to give the information and, in many ways, the aim of the lesson. This method begins to give a structure to the picture and a starting point for the qualities that need to be worked on.

2 The Breed-Chart Method

A breed chart is a simple method of presenting information about a horse's parentage, but it can also be used as a method to store and retrieve information. Like the jigsaw puzzle, each subject heading can be broken up into different components (fig. 2.2).

A novice rider probably only needs one or two headings, but as learning progresses, more can be introduced. There is a logical route to follow, which means there is more chance of committing it to memory. Coaches need to concentrate on packaging information for the needs of the person receiving it and giving her a route or method of retrieving the information.

3 The Cascading Windows

This is an arrangement of windows that overlap one another. Typically, the title bar remains visible so it is always possible to see which windows are open. The basis is simple, yet so effective. As each window is clicked upon a new level of information about the subject opens. As a greater level of information is needed, the subject expands and more depth is exposed (fig. 2.3).

Again, in coaching and teaching terms, presentation of these windows

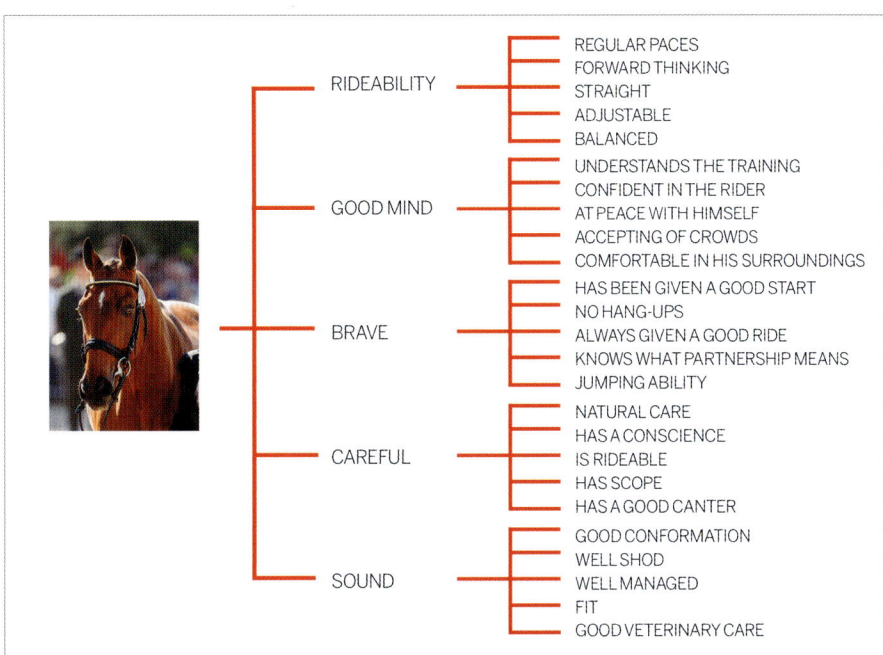

RIDEABILITY
- REGULAR PACES
- FORWARD THINKING
- STRAIGHT
- ADJUSTABLE
- BALANCED

GOOD MIND
- UNDERSTANDS THE TRAINING
- CONFIDENT IN THE RIDER
- AT PEACE WITH HIMSELF
- ACCEPTING OF CROWDS
- COMFORTABLE IN HIS SURROUNDINGS

BRAVE
- HAS BEEN GIVEN A GOOD START
- NO HANG-UPS
- ALWAYS GIVEN A GOOD RIDE
- KNOWS WHAT PARTNERSHIP MEANS
- JUMPING ABILITY

CAREFUL
- NATURAL CARE
- HAS A CONSCIENCE
- IS RIDEABLE
- HAS SCOPE
- HAS A GOOD CANTER

SOUND
- GOOD CONFORMATION
- WELL SHOD
- WELL MANAGED
- FIT
- GOOD VETERINARY CARE

2.2 Visualizing a breed chart is a simple method of storing and retrieving information.

2.3 Cascading windows open up a new level of information with every click.

needs to be tailored to the person receiving the information and how much she can or needs to take on board.

There are many methods of collating, storing, and retrieving information. These are the three that I have used that work for me. Whatever method is chosen, it must be simple in concept, easy to work with, and usable in real life.

Simple Instructions

All riders have to follow instructions: they might be delivered by a coach, written in a dressage test, or posted on a course plan. Where they come from does not matter because they are the requirements everyone must follow.

Failing to follow instructions means that, in part, you fail the test. Complying shows that you understand what is being asked of you and that you can communicate it to the horse. The horse, in turn, can then carry out the task with your help.

I begin my lessons by choosing a seemingly easy task and asking the pupil or class to execute it. "Ride a circle around me at medium walk," is an instruction I often give.

I begin by asking, "What more information do you need?" By involving riders from the outset, I am encouraging them to think about what information they require to ride a circle. They might ask what size it should be or which direction it should go in. The answers I give should then be reflected in what they do. Interestingly, this seldom happens.

> **The execution of a simple task—something that will become the foundation for all other work—has to be clearly thought about and acted upon.**

I deliberately position myself in a way that means the circle does not have an obvious boundary, so I am forcing a thought process. Once the circle is being ridden, I feed in information about the pace. I ask whether the walk/trot/canter is *forward*. I ask whether it is *regular.* By doing this I am continuing to encourage self-analysis. The circle is unlikely to be accurate, so now I am able to draw this to the rider's attention. It is interesting to watch the rider's face as she realizes her inaccuracies and irregularities, and then see how she interprets the words "forward" and "regular."

Some observers might question my technique and say that I have set the rider up for failure. I would argue the opposite. I have made her aware that the execution of a simple task—something that will become the foundation for all other work—has to be clearly thought about and acted upon. Failure to do this will undermine the attention to detail required later on to make progress.

Many tasks sound simple, but their execution is often less so. The simple tasks should be practiced until they become easy so you have a background on the learning canvas on which you can start layering on the detail.

Words and Why They Matter

There is a tendency for people within a profession to converse in their own language. Equestrianism is no different. To anyone in the outside world, "horse-speak" may as well be a foreign tongue. Even within equestrianism there are terms we use that are specific to certain disciplines. Some expressions used within show jumping may not be understood by people in the dressage world, and likewise, eventing terms can sound strange to people who show or breed horses.

There is an expression in human education called *shared understanding.* As it suggests, it is a sharing of the will to understand. This is a prerequisite to good education. Without it, education becomes one-sided and results in diminished interest and a subsequent lack of uptake. When parties want to understand, interaction produces open minds with limitless possibilities.

So often when I travel and teach, I find that the understanding of words is not clear. Not only are words misunderstood, but they are used in the wrong context and, as a result, the rider becomes horribly confused. The horse is then left best-guessing as he tries to figure out what is required of him.

As a rider, you are dealing with an animal whose brain has changed very little in thousands of years, so for you to communicate with him and expect him to understand, you must be very clear about what you want and what is in it for him—part of the *shared understanding.*

Most horses are generous by nature so will often offer a response before being asked a question. In being such willing pupils, one rider can teach a horse to do something using one aid or message, while the next rider may want the same response but use a different set of aids. This is fine until a horse changes jockeys, or a coach tries to communicate with many different horses and riders. Now there is confusion in all camps.

This is why the language a trainer or coach uses to convey instructions—whether directed at horse or rider—should be uniform and not subject to individual preferences, translations, or country choices.

Less is often more. If I save one final word to say to my pupils as they head down the centerline or leave the start box, it must make total sense. It must be unambiguous and clear. The same applies when you apply an aid—the horse must understand exactly what is being asked of him, so that one "word" makes a difference. Using the wrong word can be disastrous.

The words a coach uses must be chosen carefully and be appropriate for the level of the horse and rider's education. They must be unambiguous and convey exactly what is wanted at that time. I am forever taking pupils of all levels back to using simple words that define basic qualities so that I can reestablish their focus on the issue at hand. I also need to ensure that we are, in fact, talking about and meaning the same thing.

> **The horse must understand exactly what is being asked of him—one "word" makes a difference. Using the wrong word can be disastrous.**

Often, when people hear something they inadvertently change the wording in their minds. As they repeat it, new and different words appear—sometimes with a different meaning. Consider the story: "The general says to his aide, 'Send more trucks, we're going to advance.' By the time it gets to the soldiers it becomes, 'Send more bucks, we're going to a dance.'" It is like the game of "Telephone" (known in the United Kingdom as "Chinese Whispers"). It is easy to see how meanings can become distorted.

There are simple words, and words that mean more. Both have a time and a place. Using words that mean more too soon leads to confusion and disheartenment. Take "engagement," for example, a word that is often bandied about regardless of the stage of the horse and rider's education. Coaches talk about engagement too early. All that is really needed is an understanding of the word "forward." A true feeling of forward is as much as some riders will ever need to feel, so why use the word engagement?

To stand and watch a horse and rider working, as coaches and judges do, it is sometimes difficult to see clarity to the conversation that is going on between rider and horse. The horse's expression will often tell the story—one of confusion.

To help riders deal with this I encourage them to think about the actual qualities they want to ride and feel. These must be real, tangible, and verifiable, so they are not opinions, subjective comments, or sound-bite stuff.

With horses there are two, three, or maybe even more parties involved in producing a performance: the horse, rider, coach, veterinarian, and farrier, for example, all have their parts to play in the function of the "whole." For the whole to work at its maximum efficiency, it is vital that everyone knows what information is required and how it is stored and retrieved. The support team needs to understand the filters that avoid clogging up the passage thus slowing down the implementation of the information. This support team can be a full complement of support as in a national team, or it can be husband, wife, or friend of the amateur rider. But the horse and rider must always be on the same page; they must know what the other knows in order to perform together (fig. 2.4).

Competition horses are required to perform fairly complex tasks. Done well, the result can look and feel amazing, but when there is a communication error, the consequences can be disastrous. A good rider will guide a novice horse through a task, while an experienced horse—once he is familiar with how information from a less experienced rider is transmitted—tends to be tolerant and lower his performance to meet the new rider's expectations.

A coach needs to marry the levels and abilities of both horse and rider— shared understanding. This is a vital part of the communication between people, and without it, little is achieved.

It is almost as hard for today's coach to decide what information is *unnecessary* as what *is* necessary. We have become so used to information overload that what should be easily accessible information has become hard to find, lost in the clutter, or unable to be retrieved. The expectation from pupils to be fed high volumes of information is also an issue. Just because an instruction

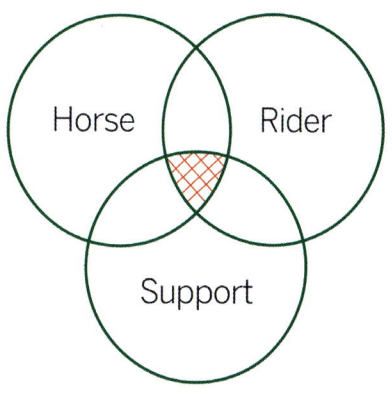

2.4 The sweet spot—where a good performance can happen.

sounds simple does not mean it is not valid. There is a developing dependence and expectation from people that in order for information to be valid it has to be complicated.

Riders and coaches need to ask to what extent this information is helpful or a burden, a distraction, confusing, or a downright hindrance (see sidebar, "The Delete Box").

The Problem with Technology

As technology becomes an increasingly important part of your life, so you become ever more dependent on it. Mobile devices and online tools provide

The Delete Box

Reprogramming the mind is an interesting process. First, it must want to be reprogrammed (see "Buying In," p. 30). Second, the unwanted information must be cleared out, and the right information fed in the correct way. I try to make the clearing-out process as humorous and light-hearted as possible: "Into the delete box, press the button, and whooosh!"

Some riders spend hours assimilating the wrong information, so for me to come along and trash it all at once can be too much to take. I want to make the rider understand why she should delete something, so I must be very clear in my reasoning.

It is important for me to give out tools to replace the ones that have been deleted, and to substitute the words that have gone into the delete box with others that can be understood. These tools and words must be simple and work for the rider in order to begin the buying-in process.

The rebuilding process thereafter must be logical. As rider and coach build the platform of information and skills, so the rider begins to see how it fits together as part of the bigger picture (see "Methods of Learning," p. 60). Simply deleting without a clear plan of with what and how the void should be filled is unproductive, but the delete box lightens and reinforces the notion that it is all right to "get rid of trash." As more layers are added, more words and expressions appear, and riders begin to trust that trash will be replaced with something valuable that follows the pattern.

an instant supply of easily accessible information to the point that if you are not in the know you run the risk of appearing backward.

To a certain extent, I believe the current equine education system has been fueled by this technological whirlwind, and it has created an even bigger gap between the rider and the horse's knowledge. Peer pressure to have the latest gadget or know-how influences minds that are still coming to terms with the world and growing up.

Coaches, too, can become whisked along in this whirlwind. They may be a source of information themselves, or feel pressured to try and keep up with it—or both. The consequences can be significant. In our haste to absorb information, we quickly develop a method of ordering it in our minds. We condense the things that we believe are important into sound bites—catchy, short collections of words that we feel cover all we need to know. If asked, we say we *know* the subject. This is called *topic jumping*. People become used to flicking backward and forward from subject to subject without retaining any knowledge. We do this on our computers by keeping open a number of tabs at any one time, so we don't need to retain information because we know exactly where we can find it. This also leads to a loss of attention span. People know where they can find subjects or instructions on their device, so they don't feel the need to remember them. I see this lack of attention span in today's lessons. I have found people to be increasingly inept at following instructions. They perform part of an exercise but leave out one vital element.

> I see a lack of attention span in today's lessons. I have found people to be increasingly inept at following instructions, performing part of an exercise but leaving out one vital element.

Short term, the sound-bite method may serve us well, but as the volume of information increases we need a filing system in our brain that allows us to retrieve information at the appropriate time. To make it work for us, this filing system—often known as *mind mapping*—needs to be practiced to enable us to recall the information quickly and when we need it.

Dexterity of the mind also needs practice, otherwise it becomes slow or ceases to function at all. It survives on a simple conditioning of routine. By exercising a neurological pathway frequently, it becomes a fast-track motorway and messages pass along it ever more quickly. When the messages

Gimmicky Gadgets

There is barely a day that goes by without my mail box being bombarded by new technological "must-haves"—gadgets that are fitted to some part of myself or my horse, and promise to transmit all the information I need to know straight to my smartphone.

Every day I take these emails and show them to my horse. When he has finished reading them I discuss the product with him to see what he thinks. Then I ask him, will a certain technological contraption help improve his centerline halt? Or tidy up his technique over a show jump? To be honest, he has difficulty seeing the merits of these products.

Yes, I might be making fun of some very worthwhile and well-intentioned pieces of equipment that *may* be of interest to some and *may* be of benefit to others. However, the bottom line is that it is only through understanding the horse and how you communicate with him that progress can be made—not through the latest piece of technology.

I do understand how important technology can be to certain aspects of the equine industry, but I caution its application.

More advanced gadgets are entering the marketplace that are even better at deciding what you should be doing, how and where you should be looking, and what you should be feeling. This is all very well until we get to a competition where our support team videos the dressage test, and the footage is stored in the phone to be compared to the other collections of data already there. What a brilliant education tool, you might think—until the dressage judge's marks do not tally with the technology. There is an outcry, "What does that judge know?" "He must be blind!" "I'm going to complain!" So the poor dressage judge gets flak for disagreeing with a smartphone!

Other sports employ a video-assistant referee to review the referee's decision. How long before dressage follows suit?

know the route they become habits looked after by the subconscious. Things happen without us having to think about them.

Life Lessons

Much of the equine-education system over the last two decades has been college-based, whether at schools devoted to horsemanship and riding instruction, or those that simply offer horse-related and agricultural classes alongside other subjects. Here, pupils could acquire a theoretical knowledge of the horse and his place in business and sport. In some countries, this has been in keeping with government guidelines applied in schools. Outcomes are measurable for both the deliverer and the pupil. It can be argued, therefore, that the outcomes run the content and delivery to retain this measurability. It is only then that it can satisfy the current trends in education. Qualifications become the outcome. Structure becomes the delivery. A satisfied system!

No.

During the last two decades the big questions in the equine industry have been, "Where do I find good staff?" and "Where is the next generation of teachers coming from?"

I had this discussion with the principal of a college that produces many hundreds of graduates every year. I explained the apparent gap in what was being taught and what skills were needed to be employable. Graduates were being taught a wide range of subjects that were not related to life within the equine industry, and they were not being given any skills that could be used. His answer was, "It is not our remit to prepare people for the workplace, but rather to give them a rounded education." A scandalous statement, and one which to my mind shows that people who are interested in horses and are willing to learn will often do much better in the industry/sport than those with school-earned qualifications. How can this be right?

Education is a subject that fascinates me. While reading around the subject, I stumbled across a scientific paper called "Battling for the Soul of Education" by John Abbott (*The NAMTA Journal*, 2015). The paper questions the current education system in light of what recent research tells us about how people learn best. It doesn't matter whether we are talking about learning in a classroom environment or learning on the back of a horse, Abbott raises some important points that all coaches should take on board. He writes:

> It is surely self-evident that the better educated people are, the less they need to be told what to do. Unfortunately, the reverse is equally true, for the less educated people are, the more government feels it necessary to issue larger rulebooks.
>
> As regulation is extended quickly it becomes self-perpetuating, for the more people accept being told what to do, the less they think for themselves. This is the tragic point that many English-speaking countries now seem to have reached; we are in danger of becoming so over-taught that we will lose the art of thinking for ourselves.

We now know that:

> **Intelligence is more than just a general capacity to learn—it is about cognitive and emotional self-regulation, the ability to apply "intelligence" in a self-reflective way.**

➤ The brain is driven by curiosity and the need to make sense of all its many experiences.

➤ Intelligence is more than just a general capacity to learn; it is shrewdness, cleverness, and knowledge all rolled together with emotional intuition, balance, and a strong sense of practicality. It is about cognitive and emotional self-regulation, the ability to apply "intelligence" in a self-reflective way.

➤ Learning is an immensely complex business, so to put faith in a highly directive, prescriptive curriculum is to so go "against the grain of the brain," that it inhibits creativity and enterprise—the very skills needed in the complex, diverse economy and community for which we need to prepare the next generation.

CHAPTER THREE

Coaching Now and Then

Many of the great equestrian coaches came from (and continue to come from) a cavalry background, where the education of horse and rider had a more serious purpose—that of preparing for war. After the wars, these wonderful horsemen continued to ply their trade in a more peaceful way, educating civilian riders and sport horses. They brought with them structure, discipline, and a wealth of experience to the evolving sport of riding. They had a maturity that afforded them authority and a certain presence. Most were comfortable with themselves, which also allowed them humor. The likes of Jack Le Goff and Bert de Némethy have untold legacies in today's sport.

Coaching qualifications have evolved over the years: how lessons are prepared and delivered has changed, and what pupils expect is also different. Awareness of safety has greatly improved.

My British Horse Society (BHS) training has stayed with me throughout my career: every lesson should have a start, middle, and an end. It should be structured. I have words of command that allow me to move people around without thinking. This leaves me free to concentrate on the content of the lesson. I am practiced in doing drill rides with classes, which can be of huge benefit to horse and rider.

Without this structure to my earlier training, I would have found it so much harder to deliver later on. Coaches need to be adaptable, creative, and realistic. At times, they must be the bad guy, and at other times, the good guy. They need to explore the minds of horse and rider, and find a way in to enable all parties to have *shared understanding.*

Coaches need to be adaptable, creative, and realistic.

Learn from Doing

From the "do as I say" approach of yesteryear, coaching has now become much more inclusive and interactive. Pupils are now asked, "Did you notice the difference?" "How does that feel?" "What do you think happens now?" This is a great improvement. Sometimes, however, the pendulum swings too far and there becomes an overdependence on "the chat"! Instructors and coaches can talk too much, explain too much, feel the need to hear their own voice too much. The lesson then becomes a theoretical dialogue rather than a "doing" process.

When this happens pupils can often miss opportunities to learn from doing. There is also the risk that they will feed off the coach, and in doing so, no longer think for themselves. They become coach-dependent. There is an increasing need for riders to take *responsibility for themselves.* Otherwise, it is like traveling by GPS: you are never quite sure where you are, where you've been, what you've seen or experienced on the way, and can certainly never find your way back!

> **A lesson learned is better than a lesson taught.**

Coaches need to be careful they do not lose the skills they are taught in early training: voice control, words of command, open and closed questions, class movements, drill rides, and lesson structure. Not being familiar with some of these can limit what can be achieved in a lesson. These early lessons remain a valuable part of my toolbox and I use them to illustrate subjects, retain control, focus on imparting the right information, and have fun.

I sometimes listen to coaches at competitions in wonderment. The words they use are seldom for the benefit of the pupil—more often for the consumption of those listening. In many cases, there is no way the pupil understands or is capable of doing what is being asked of her. What a waste of money and time!

We must never lose sight of the pupil's part in learning and the trainer's role in facilitating this—not just teaching. *A lesson learned is better than a lesson taught.* It requires a different approach and, often, different skills.

Riding is unlike any other sport because development has to encompass the horse's needs and desires, as well as the rider's. Coaches need to blend all the detail necessary to teach skills to both horse and rider, but also understand the bigger picture and how to guide and mentor the duo to realize their potential.

For this reason, it is important not to get drawn into too many examples of how other sports do things. It is fine to look and see if some coaching techniques can be adapted and become interchangeable, but in many cases they cannot, so beware.

Definitions

Why are there so many different ways of riding? This is a fair question to ask. Should everyone not ride in the same or a similar way? When couples dance

The Problem with Having Multiple Trainers

How should you choose who helps you? Often, you might not get it right the first time.

After a lesson, you should feel you were important to the coach, you liked the message and how it was delivered, and enjoyed the empathy between the coach, yourself, and the horse. You should feel challenged. You should have had fun.

All the above would encourage you to go back again; however, many people choose to ignore this. There can be many reasons—some valid, some most certainly not.

Many parents with children who ride get drawn down the road of having multiple coaches—fashionable trainers with loud voices. Ultimately, the result is a confused rider.

There is a saying that you can learn something from everyone. It is true, so long as you understand what it is coaches are trying to do in the first place, and you can appreciate an alternative view. Without this understanding, the result is confusion all round.

Some riders want a change, but in switching between trainers find themselves stuck between two philosophies and unable to clarify the right direction in their own mind. Then it becomes difficult for the rider to impart the information to the horse.

together the movements are fundamentally the same; however, there are differences in style and detail, depending on where in the world you are.

Let me begin by clarifying some of the words that describe teaching. I am conscious that these words and their definitions differ from country to country, but their roles are largely the same.

What is the difference between a coach, instructor, and a trainer? For the purpose of this book, I have used the generic term "coach" to cover all

Learning from Barrel Racing

A few years ago, I was teaching a clinic in Washington State and found out that Nicole Aichele, the World-Record-holder at the time in the popular American sport of barrel racing, lived only a few miles away. Curious to find out more about this horse sport, in which a horse and rider attempt to complete a cloverleaf pattern around preset barrels in the fastest time, I set up a meeting with Nicole. I spent an amazing few hours in her company, and had a chance to ride her World-Record-winning partner, Blondie.

The encounter left me thinking how much we had in common despite our disciplines seemingly being worlds apart—she, a 20-something-year-old barrel racer and me, a 60-something-year-old eventer.

This is what Nicole wrote afterward: "I have just spent an enjoyable two hours giving Eric a lesson in my sport, barrel racing. The thing that struck me most throughout the session was the common ground we both shared in terms of our language and what we wanted from our horses. We were using the same words and asking our horses for the same skills, yet our sports were so different.

"As the lesson went on it became apparent that our disciplines were not so far apart after all: the level of horsemanship we strive for is very similar. I want my horse to be light to my aid, to think for himself, and to be in balance. I want him to enjoy what he is doing and participate in it willingly."

Nicole has promised to reciprocate the challenge and bring one of her young barrel-racing horses to a jumping clinic. It will be a fascinating lesson.

the other words that describe this profession. In reality, though, it is not that simple, however much we try to make it so. During the last 10 to 15 years, the use and interpretation of the words *coach, instructor,* and *trainer* have evolved to reflect changes in how these roles are viewed and their position in modern sport.

Coach

Dictionary definition: "A person involved in the direction, instruction, and training of the operations of a sports team or of individual sportspeople."

A coach may also be a teacher, and while understanding and often being very competent at all roles, a coach is often one step removed from the process of actually teaching the detail. The coach's main role is to take a holistic view on things.

> There is a link between all the disciplines: They may have different goals, but they should have common principles.

Instructor

Dictionary definition: "A person whose job it is to teach someone a skill."

Traditionally, a riding instructor was also responsible for managing feeding, training, competition programs, the horse and rider before and after the show, and future plans. Now, many of these duties have been taken over by specialists, which, in turn, make the instructor's role more specialized. The instructor must ensure there is a progressive program of training and that all the pieces of the jigsaw are in place. Each piece is either a skill or the link between skills.

Trainer

Dictionary definition: "Someone who teaches."

In equestrian terms, this means the trainer teaches either the horse or the rider, or both together.

Coaching Across Boundaries

I am often asked whether I teach eventing, dressage, or jumping. The perception is that to just teach "riding" is for lesser instructors and to teach dressage or show jumping requires much more knowledge—something only a specialist coach can deliver.

Why do people think it is not possible to teach all these three main English riding disciplines up to any level? When I answer the teaching question, I try to make it clear there is a link between all the disciplines. There may be different goals, but there should be common principles. Finding this common ground is an important starting point for all coaches. Without it, each discipline finds its own route and there becomes a danger of reinventing the wheel.

Two qualities are always present no matter what you are asking horses to do: *control of direction* and *control of speed*—that is, controlling *line* and *pace*. From trail riding to polo, racing to dressage, vaulting to barrel racing, all require control of these two fundamentals.

When you start with this in common, it becomes easier to bring the disciplines closer together in how to achieve these qualities. We all want a horse that is a nice riding animal—an animal that is physically and mentally easy to manage, a self-starter that goes by himself, and is "forward" in his mind. An easy riding horse also has to accept and understand the rider's aids in order for him to do and go where he is asked. These are called start points (see p. 69) and without these, you cannot begin.

Todd, Nicholson, and Tait

When competing at a championship some years ago, I went down to the warm-up area to see what was going on. I arrived to find three New Zealand riders doing the same thing, just watching. They were three of the greatest riders in the last 30 years: Mark Todd, Andrew Nicholson, and Blyth Tait. I have since nicknamed them "TNT." We chatted and I asked them why they were here watching rather than back at the accommodation socializing. In unison, they replied, "We might learn something."

This attitude is part of the reason for their success. They watched, saw, thought about, and implemented their findings. This attitude only works if the "thought" part has a foundation of knowledge, a start point, as this then avoids confusion.

The Need for Success

All sport, whether undertaken for pleasure or as a profession, tends to get swept along with the tide of the time. You need to decide and be comfortable with the reason you ride in the first place—is it for fun, pleasure, exercise, the feeling of two minds interacting, or competition? Success is looked upon as something to be copied, but it can be measured in many ways: the good guys must be doing something right, so we should follow them and do the same.

The more professional a sport becomes the more emphasis is placed on success: sports' managers lose their jobs if they don't produce results, athletes are under constant pressure to perform, and people in the workplace have targets to meet. There seems no end to the need for success; it seems we are driven by this need to improve, to be successful. But success can be a misguided driving force. Success can also be just having fun, staying on board, enjoying the experience of horses.

Success is looked upon as something to be copied, but it can be measured in many ways.

"I want to be famous," says the television talent contestant. I would argue that saying, "I want to be the best I can," is a far more constructive ambition because not only are you striving to better yourself—a path that may lead to fame anyway—but you are also heading for a more satisfying existence. Being the best you can in our sport also requires you to understand the horse's brain—to apply this same logic with horses, so that they also can be the best *they* can.

CHAPTER FOUR

How Horses Learn

have already outlined various methods of learning that have been useful to me (see Methods of Learning, p. 6), but what about the horse? How easy it would be if you could just show him a video and say, "This is how I want you to go."

To help horses learn and achieve, you must know what you want and how you can explain it to them. We have always been taught that horses learn by repetition, but I am not sure people always understand the hows and whys of this statement. Just doing something often does not, in itself, make it better. It is only when a task is done well and done often that it becomes good. This is called a *conditioned reflex.*

It is only when a task is done well and done often that it becomes good.

"Do it right—do it often—it becomes a good habit. Recall the habit often—it becomes a good instinct."

"A lesson learned is more likely to last than a lesson taught."

"Practice perfect makes perfect practice."

"Stimulate curiosity and learning happens by itself."

These well-known clichés are common and valid, but it would be more helpful to know *why* they work and *how* to put them into practice.

Let us look a little more closely at the process.

Humans have the ability to watch and copy, as do animals. Humans also have the ability to think *how* and *why,* and *what* the outcome might be. Horses do not. The horse responds to your input, but he is not like you: he does not understand the hows and whys, or that there is a progressive training process that will take the partnership to an end result. You should not assume the horse will reason or understand what you want—to do so may lead to disappointment.

Intelligence is defined as the ability to reason. Sometimes, when it comes to simple tasks that are in their interest, horses do reason, but their intelligence is not like yours. They live and think in the moment.

Create a Learning Pathway

As the horse is given a stimulus—for example, a simple "move forward" request from the leg—if he chooses the correct response and moves forward, you give him a reward, confirming that he has made a good choice. By doing this, your create an important link both from yourself to the horse's mind and from the horse's mind to your body. A neurological pathway has been created.

But what if the horse chooses the wrong option? A pathway that leads to a crossroads or junction could prompt an incorrect decision.

To prevent this happening, you repeat the same stimulus and, when the correct response is produced again, the pathway becomes more familiar and easier to navigate.

This neurological process produces a substance called *myelin*, which wraps itself around the nerve that is delivering the message and insulates it. This insulation helps the message travel faster. The more the pathway is used, the more insulated it becomes, so the faster the message travels down the motorway, and as a result, the horse's reflex becomes quicker.

Warm Up the Body, Switch On the Brain

When I talk about warming up, people's eyes light up in recognition. This is where the warm-up of muscles happens, just like the human athlete! It is where you stretch and supple and increase the horse's circulation to help him do the tasks you are about to ask of him.

This is what we are taught and it sounds very logical, but I look at in a different way.

When the blind man's guide dog has his harness put on, he is immediately on duty. There is no warm-up. If a guide dog needed time to wind up into work mode, the blind man would be put at risk.

We know that horses learn by repetition. They learn both good and bad things this way—they have no measure of what is correct except when you tell them. As I watch people warm up, I see horses on a long rein being allowed to be hollow, fall in or out, and perform sloppy transitions. Then after 10 minutes the horse is encouraged to come into a shape and work more correctly.

Is this not a waste of 10 minutes and a contradiction to learning by repeating good practice?

A horse in his natural environment is ready to take flight at any time. He can go from zero to 30 mph to get away from danger, doing himself no harm whatsoever. You take a horse out of the stable where he has been for 12 hours and turn him out in the field, only to watch him buck, squeal, and gallop. So warming up the muscles is not the priority. Yes, muscles must be warmed up, ligaments need stretching, and the athlete prepared, but the priority is to immediately engage the brain with an acceptance and understanding of the aid. Just like the guide dog.

> **Most important in the warm-up is that the horse's mind is with the rider and attentive.**

This point was nicely illustrated at the International Eventing Forum in 2015, where Olympic medalist and 2017 Badminton winner Andrew Nicholson rode four horses in quick succession during his presentation. When he was asked who was warming up his next horse, he replied, "No one. Horses need to get used to switching on quickly."

How much better would it be if horses were conditioned to think, "Tack on, accept" and "Tack off, I'm off duty"? This is very clear to all. As the rider gets on, the horse thinks, "I'm ready and listening, what now?"

The response is only a matter of conditioning the mind of the rider and horse. Of course, I am not advocating jumping 5 feet (1.50 m) or asking for piaffe in the first few minutes—or indeed demanding that you should expect good work immediately. The first 10 to 20 minutes should comprise simple exercises to test forwardness, straightness, and regular paces.

I have watched riders try to get their horse "on the bit" for 20 minutes or more. As they struggle, so it becomes the focus of their hour's riding. This must be so tedious and what a waste of time! When I question them why it is taking so long, I am often told, "He always takes time to accept the bit."

From the beginning, the horse's acceptance should be correct, but not demanding, so the muscles are being used in the right way and developed accordingly. Most important, however, is that the horse's mind is with the rider and attentive. Is it not logical to make sure that all the "controls" work as you start your ride? So check.

CHAPTER FIVE

The Young Horse

I avoid using the expression "breaking in" young horses; I "start" my horses. I understand the principle of "breaking something in"—that of disassembling it and rebuilding it in a way that suits uniformity. There is sometimes merit in doing this, especially when the mind can understand why and see the results, but in most (unfortunately, still not all) cases, the training of the horse is about establishing a partnership, so "breaking in" is a flawed expression.

"Do as I say" should always be followed by the word "because." This encourages the horse to join in with the process. I call this "buying in." You will read this expression throughout this book. It is the way I like to encourage riders and horses to work together. I want them to *buy in* to the process and become part of it.

From the very start with young horses, I show and reward an interest in their learning. I want them to be individuals, fully aware of what they are doing because they understand and want to be involved. In human sports psychology, you will hear about the benefits of an engaged mind. It is no different with a horse.

Accepting what is being taught should lead to understanding, therefore, the process of accepting must be clear from the outset. Boundaries must be put in place because without these, there is no structure to the partnership.

Understanding a horse's natural instincts is fundamental to this process. We all know that horses are animals of fight or flight and that they learn by repetition. When put in a situation where there is no obvious escape route, they will fight their corner. But by understanding these instincts, it is possible

> **"Do as I say" should always be followed by the word "because."**

to avoid the behaviors you don't want to produce and nurture the ones that are helpful. A horse in the stable has no obvious escape route. You are in his territory and you need to be invited in. Once a horse has opened his mind to your being there, provided you are non-aggressive, he is likely to quietly accept you moving around him, grooming him, handling him, or tidying the bed. As he takes an interest in you, he is *buying in* to what you are doing.

> **The horse has a right to expect that you will be consistent every time you ask something of him.**

This philosophy continues as you tack up and begin handling the horse as part of the starting process. The horse has a right to expect that you will be consistent every time you ask something of him. Every time his halter is put on, or the saddle and bridle appear, the horse needs to *buy in* to a positive interaction with you and be interested in what is happening. Note: Sometimes, people use treats to engage the horse in this process. This is fine, but beware the horse that expects a treat and nips when it does not appear.

As a horse's education progresses, it is important to know his character. Some need teaching slowly, others will pick things up quickly. Some are shy, some are pushy, some want to please, while others are not sure if they have done the right thing. A reward is crucial to the process, and as long as the horse's answer is on the correct lines, it should always be rewarded. These positive, reinforcing gestures encourage the horse to follow where you are going. He will soon start to look and anticipate what is coming next and, although he may not always get it right, he will continue to *buy in* to the process. These positive actions are developing the good, clear neurological pathways that are so vital to establishing a strong partnership.

Reward and Reprimand

Horses are very receptive to praise in the form of patting and an encouraging voice. They also know they have not performed well when the rider "growls" and/or gives a sharp nudge of the leg aid. The "reprimand" must be appropriate to the character of the horse receiving it, and I believe it is important to be demonstrative at both ends of the scale so the horse is quite clear what constitutes good and bad responses and behavior.

Partnership vs Dictatorship

Where in this wide world can man find nobility without pride,
friendship without envy, or beauty without vanity?
Here where grace is laced with muscle and strength by gentleness confined.

He serves without servility; he has fought without enmity.
There is nothing so powerful, nothing less violent;
there is nothing so quick, nothing more patient.

England's past has been borne on his back.
All our history is in his industry.
We are his heirs;
He is our inheritance.

"The Horse" by Ronald Duncan ©
(Copyright of) the Ronald Duncan Estate

It is important to understand the word "partnership" and how it relates to equestrian sport. The dictionary definition of partnership is, "Where two individuals work together for a common cause." But I like to add in a few words and define it this way: "Where two individuals, *each fully understanding their role,* work together for a common cause."

This definition clearly describes a relationship where two parties willingly, and with full understanding, work together for a cause or to advance their interests.

But what is the horse's interest? What is his cause? Is it possible for a horse to have full understanding? Maybe not. So is the word "partnership" correct to describe the relationship? It is certainly not a "dictatorship" where an individual directs or commands others to follow her will. I like partnership and all that it entails better. Clearly, though, it is not possible for a horse to have an understanding of progressive training, the requirements of a dressage test, or the design of a jumping course, so the majority of the responsibility falls on you. You must be clear about where the responsibility lies in the unequal relationship that forms a horse-rider partnership.

This is all part of the challenge and intrigue that makes riding such an intellectual tease. How do you encourage the horse to follow your logic and where it might take you? Why should he do what you are asking, *buy in*, and embrace it all with enthusiasm?

The horse has every right to ask what is in it for him.

Human athletes continually break records by pushing the limit of their ability further and further. Yet the speed of the equine derby winner has not become faster for a hundred years or more in spite of improved training techniques, veterinary care, feeding knowledge, and racecourse ground maintenance.

Why?

The horse cannot, for obvious reasons, see any benefit in pushing himself through the pain barrier for greater benefit. It does not matter to our grass-eater whether he wins Olympic gold or bags one million in prize money. His life remains unaltered.

The only reason that a horse joins your partnership is his generosity of spirit: a spirit that has to be nurtured, cherished, applauded, loved, and never taken for granted.

> The only reason that a horse joins your partnership is his generosity of spirit: a spirit that has to be nurtured, cherished, applauded, loved, and never taken for granted.

With partnership comes responsibility, and the trust that the other member of the team is doing his or her bit for the good of the relationship and in pursuit of a common goal. This is another instance where there is the potential for unequal sides. It is easy for the rider to blame the horse for not doing the right thing but not so easy for the horse to tell the rider when she falls short.

This is one of the difficulties that it is important to explore. How do you make a partnership work?

Progressive training is a series of steps that logically follow one another to build upon a foundation that is understood and secure. In the end, you are left with a picture of the complete jigsaw puzzle, the finished article. Along the way the horse is entrusted with responsibility. He is rewarded when he

Welcome to the Horse House

There is no obvious way into the "Horse House" (fig. 5.1). There are doors, windows, skylights, and even a chimney, but on first glance they all appear to be locked. It is important that you gain access, as once inside, you can discuss with the horse what happens next and where you want to go. This is how you can influence an outcome or change a reaction.

To force your way into the Horse House is counterproductive, so any indication of a willingness to invite you in should be welcomed—the offer of a foot in the front door is a good start. As the horse becomes more comfortable with the initial discussion, the front door will open wider and further discussion can take place. The horse might only tolerate a partial opening of the front door at this stage in his training, but there is no harm in trying to explore a different way in—a window, down the chimney, through the terrace doors, or the kitchen door. A collection of partial welcomes and acceptances will soon allow entrance, and once in the living room, discussion and negotiation can take place. Eventually, when mutual trust is established, you may get asked in and to stay for dinner.

5.1 Welcome to the Horse House....

Many coaches will claim that their way into the Horse House is right, but the bottom line is that *any* way into the Horse House is acceptable, provided it is fair to the horse. You must not force your way in as this may jeopardize the partnership you are trying to build for the future. Eventually, you will be invited in the front door as a friend.

A horse that is left with his integrity and character, yet is willing to accommodate your views and desires, becomes a good partner—one that is prepared to put himself out to please and work toward your goal.

With an educated and exploring mind, both coach and rider will find many ways into the Horse House. Once in, a secure partnership can develop and flourish.

grasps this and produces a result when asked. In certain situations, the horse must make decisions for himself. The trainer has the responsibility of guiding him in what is right or wrong, or suggesting what he could do better, but must not take responsibility away from the horse because then the partnership becomes a dictatorship. It is a fine line that is often difficult to define.

When the rider makes a mistake or does a less-than-perfect job, the horse has to be generous enough to forgive and move on. The rider has to be the partnership's conscience—a difficult role, as people do not like to blame themselves. It is far easier to pass the blame elsewhere—often to the horse. Riders are, nevertheless, taught to take the blame. "The horse is only doing what you ask." "You weren't clear in your explanation." "You gave the wrong aid." And so on. But when the horse does make a mistake or doesn't take responsibility for an action that was clearly his, you must be able to call your partner out on it (see Reward and Reprimand, p. 31). True partnerships work because there is respect for each partner's ability to do his or her job. There is an understanding that says no offense is taken when one partner flags up that the other is falling short of what is expected.

The Right Foundations

Often, you spend as much time with your horses as you do your spouse, so it should come as no surprise that they become a reflection of you and who you are—scary, but true! The relationship that develops over time between horse and rider is reflected in how both parties work together.

There continues to be discussion on the influences of nurture and nature in an animal's development. Much is written on the hard-wiring of genetics and how "it is what it is," while research has also looked at soft-wiring. What are the influences of parents immediately after the birth of their offspring? And to what extent does this affect the chemical balance that is evolving in the developing youngster's makeup?

When it comes to horses, we know the dam has a great influence and we have all heard stories of how an orphan foal's behavior is different than it might have been with a normal upbringing. My mares have certainly stamped their progeny. I find it intriguing to watch their relationship: the foal, continually testing boundaries and then pushing them; and the mother, explaining these boundaries and then enforcing them.

At all times, the mare is the secure, central figure. She shows goodness and consistency. When you start to take over the role of parent, it is important that you, too, display these qualities. This is not only true with foals and young horses, but new partnerships with older horses also rely on this dynamic.

Smart

Think of the acronym **SMART**:
Simple
Measurable
Achievable
Realistic
Targets

Think long term; visualize the finished article. Understand that on your way to reaching the goal, there will be twists, turns, and steps backward. Trust the building blocks and pieces of the jigsaw puzzle. One may fall out and need to be replaced many times before it eventually stays put.

This is why it is vital to have a method to clarify the route forward.

Groundwork

Groundwork is not only useful for young horses; there are benefits for horses of all ages. But before undertaking this type of work, it is important to know what you are trying to achieve and how it can be done.

At every point of contact with the horse, there needs to be a set standard for the behavior you expect. Consistency will reap rewards. I walk in a brisk way, so I expect my horse to walk in from the field in a brisk way (figs. 5.2 A & B). When I ask my horse to move over in the aisle, lift up his legs, load

A

5.2 A & B If you accept A, the horse is unlikely to give you B.

into a vehicle, or step back when I give him his food, I want him to respond in a crisp and clean manner. This expectation must be transmitted to the horse clearly, in a way that the horse doesn't feel intimidated by, but accepts as an understood reaction.

I try to be the same with people. My students quickly catch on that when I say things clearly, I do not expect a reply of, "What?" or, "Could you say that again?" If I say, "Whole ride...*trot,*" for example, the trot must happen immediately on the word of command.

The word "discipline" has become misrepresented in today's language in families, schools, in the work place, in sport, and in life in general. For me, it means "boundaries" and the understanding that there is a need to adhere to these.

In training the horse, you must define what is acceptable and what is not. In adhering to the same boundaries, you are able to create a structure to your interaction—a reflection of what, I believe, should be present in society in general. By enforcing these boundaries, you need to be conscious of the individual and his character: for the sensitive horse it must a subtle reminder, but for

The Reprimand

In the 20 years I rode my most successful event horse, Enterprise, I think I only tapped him with my whip three times, such was his sensitivity. The first time was as a young horse when he stopped at the first jump in his first event—I got dumped! The second time was going into the water at his first Badminton—he was mortified that I had doubted him, and I apologized with a pat. The third time was at the 1996 Summer Olympics in Atlanta, when I said sorry as I was doing it.

I tell this story because it is important to point out that in enforcing boundaries, you do not need to resort to corporal punishment. The reprimand, punishment, or reminder must be appropriate for the character receiving it. A growl or voice noise was always enough for Enterprise to know what I needed of him. This is part of the boundary mindset.

the less sensitive individual, it can be more robust. In both cases, individuals must know that a boundary exists because then there is more effort made to comply. This effort is reinforcement of a good work ethic.

Stable Manners

Once the horse accepts you entering his space and moving around, the next stage is for you to be able to move *him* around. This should be done with a halter and lead rope, and from both sides to ensure an evenness of input.

By touching his sides where the leg aid would be applied, it is possible to simulate the application of the leg. Move the horse away from the hand, using the voice to reinforce the request. The responses you accept can be graded depending on the horse's age and level of education. I would expect a more educated horse to move to a lighter aid, hold himself in better balance, and understand more where he is putting his feet compared to a three-year-old.

Leading

When leading a horse, it is important to encourage him to walk by himself with you at his shoulder. Doing so equally from both sides from a young age will improve your chances of producing a straight riding horse. Practice halts and trot-offs as these are good for showing off a horse and for vets' visits. Both should be a normal part of his daily routine.

The signals the handler gives, when done at *every* point of contact, will reinforce the riding aids. When asking a horse to stop and stand, the stop might not happen immediately, and the halt might not last for more than a few seconds, but both must happen. As the horse's learning progresses, the response time can be sped up and the halt encouraged to last longer. It is simple stuff but it all leads to the horse *buying in* to the process.

Stepping Back

By using the voice and tapping your foot on the horse's foot, you will find that he is happy to move away from the pressure. Reward him and then walk forward. A simple exercise like this confirms understanding or an introduction to a new understanding. It is time well spent.

Competition Longeing

If you feel your horse might also benefit from longeing at a competition (see more longeing on p. 42), it is important to ask yourself:

➤ Does my horse longe?

➤ Can I longe?

➤ When I longe my horse at home, is it constructive?

➤ Am I going to be the one to longe the horse at a competition? If not, does my helper know how to longe?

What do you want the horse to do on the longe? Nothing more than when you are riding him. You should be striving for the same qualities: forwardness, straightness, regularity, balance, and the acceptance and understanding of the aids. Longeing must be a part of the progressive training process. It must also make sense to the horse—there should be a link to what you ask for after the longeing. This is often lacking.

The horse's conformation needs to be taken into consideration as certain shapes respond to certain techniques. Certain extra pieces of equipment, when used correctly and conscientiously, can help achieve the desired result. Note that there are full books written on gadgets and training aids. I have heard it said that "gadgets should be left to the experts, but the experts don't need them!" They are *never* a shortcut and are not a magic answer, and their use must be fully understood or left well alone.

In deciding what—if anything—you need, it is important to have a working knowledge of what each piece of equipment does and how it may or may not influence different horses and their way of going. It is crucial to always look at the acceptance of the gadget. Just because it has the capability of forcing the horse into a position does not mean that the horse understands why he is being put there. A proper introduction to the equipment is important, where the horse is allowed time to get used to it, and this should always happen at home, not at a competition.

I have had success using the following training aids. Used correctly and with understanding they have been most helpful.

Side-Reins

These are designed to encourage the horse onto a contact and give the feel of what the rider's hands might feel like. They are not to position the shape of the head/neck. Side-reins are often abused! Fixing the horse in a certain shape can be counterproductive as the horse can learn ways to avoid using himself correctly. Remember, just because the horse looks to be in the correct shape does not mean that he is working properly.

Chambon

Another piece of equipment that is often misused (fig. 5.3). The chambon is there to encourage a correct way of going, *not* to force a horse to put his head and/or neck down!

5.3 The chambon can encourage a correct way of going, but must never force an outline.

5.4 A Market Harborough has its place, as it can help give the rider a feel for what it takes to ride a horse on the bit.

Think of it as showing a good way, while discouraging a poor way. In doing this, you are reinforcing a conditioned reflex or habit of doing it correctly. When the horse holds the bit or demonstrates tension, it does not matter where his head/neck position is, the chambon is having no effect. Longe first and then *remove* the chambon before riding.

Market Harborough

This is another piece of equipment that is often misunderstood—restriction is *not* the aim (fig. 5.4). Security of contact can be the benefit, and it can be very helpful to give a horse the understanding of an outline. It can also be extremely helpful to give the rider a feel for what it takes to ride a horse on the bit, in a frame, or in an outline. Often, while learning this skill, riders become too busy and inconsistent with their hands, with the result

being a horse that becomes annoyed or irritated by the process. This then becomes counterproductive. When the Market Harborough is introduced for a limited period of time, and used well, it can be most helpful.

Anyone who is likely to longe the horse at a competition should have practiced what to do and how to do it, so it requires a team effort and involvement to ensure there are no sudden changes on the day. And a note about sport longeing: This is designed to encourage horses to let off steam! It is best done without a saddle as you do not want to give the horse the impression that bucking with a saddle on is acceptable. It can be a double-edged sword, as just enough sport longeing can be very beneficial, but too much can often wind a horse up and make him more excited. Boots and a bridle are helpful.

All exercises out of the stable should be done with the horse's tack on because you are then creating an association between tack, attention to the human, and what certain movements mean. This is good reinforcement of your "right" to request from the horse. By layering more onto this foundation before we get on board, the movements begin to have an association with riding and will be easier to achieve from the saddle.

Longeing

The art of longeing can be a delight, as watching the horse from the ground gives a different perspective of what is going on and, as a rider, what you need to be doing to make it better. Understanding the possible solutions and being

My Youngsters at Four

My two young horses have continued to remind me how good things can pop up when you least expect them, yet how important it is to seize these moments and make the most of them.

On one occasion, my four-year-old mare, who was quite an introvert, gave me the most wonderful transition from one gait to another, which I would have been pleased to feel from an advanced horse. I had no idea where it came from because, until then, she hadn't shown any recognition of the balance required or acceptance of the aids to make this happen.

I made her very aware how good she had been and then we carried on. Nothing like that feeling appeared again that day, or

in subsequent days.

My gelding of the same age had other things going on. To him, leg pressure meant anything—from "nothing" to "go faster." Neither was correct, but he was coming to terms with me being keen to converse with him with the leg. Every now and then he understood, and then his mind went elsewhere and he couldn't multi-task. He was like a gawky teenage boy!

I continually tried to put him in a situation where he needed my leg input, like riding up and down gentle hills, negotiating trot poles and turns. Then I could "talk" to him with my leg and he began to get the message. When he ran away I tried not to slow him down with my hand, but to use turns or distractions to make him rebalance himself. Now my leg is there and able to implement them can be very rewarding; to see a result right in front of you gives a horseman a real buzz.

I enjoy watching how horses develop their way of going from the ground and how, with careful choice of exercises, you can help improve their biomechanics. Longeing is not just for young horses; older horses relish it and doing work without the rider can improve their way of going.

There are many different gadgets that can be used for longeing, but the overriding proviso is that handling of the equipment must be instinctive to you, so you can focus solely on what the horse is doing. Otherwise, it can become dangerous. It is important to remember that not only does the horse need to be trained to longe, but training yourself to do the longeing is equally crucial.

able to chat to him, and at the same time he has slowed himself down.

By applying an aid, even if it is apparently not yet understood, I was tapping at the door in both my horses' minds and, at some stage, that door will open (see Horse House, p. 34). By being aware of this and rewarding the horse, I sowed a seed, so that later on when I arrived at this subject again, the horse thought, "I know what that means," and gave a good response. This is a secure start point.

Being aware of what young horses can suddenly produce out of nowhere is part of the fun and intrigue of piecing together the jigsaw puzzle, but do not be fooled into believing these flashes are the norm or secure—they are not. The journey dips in and out of all sorts of issues. As much as you want to believe that a youngster will retain a piece of information or a skill at the first time of asking, it won't happen. But it is important to keep filling in the gaps on page 1 even though one or two pieces have appeared on pages 3, 5, and 10. It is a process of continually securing the simple, basic building blocks while welcoming and rewarding the flashes to the future that appear.

The meandering road to becoming educated needs direction and boundaries. Knowing where it is going and what is acceptable enables you to continually stage-manage the building blocks. My gawky boy was easily distracted, while my apparently attentive girl seemed to take it all in. They both progressed well; they just learned different things at different times along the same road.

Young Horse Vocabulary

Many people reading this book will never take any part in the production of a young horse and will, instead, leave it to the professional to start off their horse. I believe, however, that it is valuable for all riders to have some insight into the process as it helps to understand where the horse has got to in his education, and appreciate that it is an ongoing process that is seldom finished. Assuming that horses "know" things can be unfair on both parties and will lead to confusion in the process of progressive training.

The horse goes through many stages on his way to becoming educated. In the beginning, even conforming to simple wishes can seem like quite a trauma for him. His uncertainty of what you want him to do is sometimes a "best guess" and getting it right doesn't always happen. When it does happen, it may not always be acknowledged at the right time for him to know that it was correct. His learning can be a game of trial and error.

On the other side of this educational game, riders need to know what they want to happen, how to ask for it, and what the likely outcomes will be given the stage of training of the horse. The horse needs to be helped with his "best guess."

I remind myself of this every time I start a young horse or begin retraining an older one: simple, clear input and limited expectation.

Sometimes, you may think that what you ask for is simple, but it may not be so. For example, when you ask a horse to go on the line you want, the horse has no idea that there is such a thing as a line, let alone how important it is. He will be satisfied that he is going in a desired direction. It is just the same when you ask a horse to "take me forward." He has no comprehension of what pace is required. He will be satisfied that he is actually going somewhere.

In the beginning, you should understand this simplicity of response and learn to mold and guide it in the direction you ultimately want. This guiding and molding can only progress as the horse becomes more accepting and understanding of the aids. This takes time and a belief that it will happen. Young horses often go through a stage of running faster when the leg is applied, believing it is the response the rider wants, or being numb to the

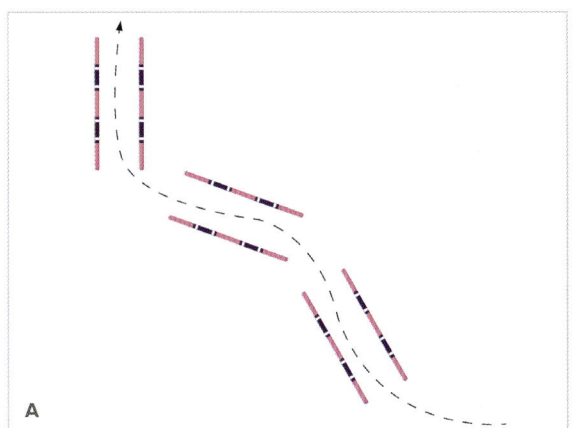

A

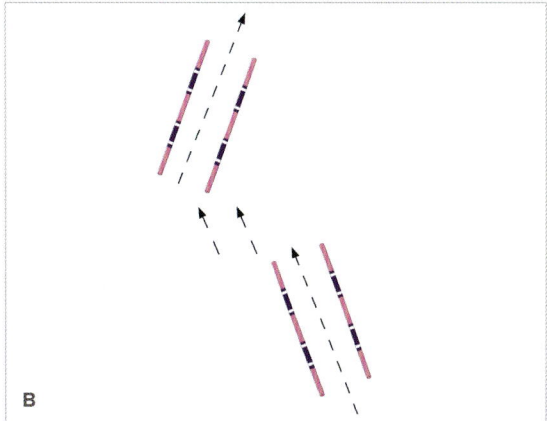

B

leg, believing that this is the response that signifies acceptance. Eventually, the horse will understand that you are trying to carry on a conversation with him. When this happens, the leg can start to mean, "hold that line" or "move over," with continued feedback from you when it's right so his tolerance to the request grows. By repeating the good, and rewarding the horse accordingly, his understanding of what he is being asked deepens. Simple ground pole exercises are really useful to help clarify the aids (figs. 5.5 A & B).

5.5 A & B A simple pole exercise as in A can be really useful to first check and then reinforce the horse's understanding of the leg and rein aids. By arranging the two sets of parallel poles like in B, you can introduce the idea that the leg means "Move over" to encourage the horse to step sideways.

CHAPTER SIX

The Inappropriate Partner

There are many reasons why we end up with the horses we do. "He was cheap!" or "I bred him," are among the common ones. It is our decision to own a horse: we do not have to; we could be doing something else. But the fact we choose riding as a hobby gives us the right to choose the partner we share it with. This quickly becomes a very emotive subject and one that I am often advised not to comment on, but I feel it is important to address, not least for the welfare of the horse.

As a coach, I do not always have the choice of whom I teach. People I do not know book lessons, sign up for clinics, and join my classes. The uncertainty of who turns up is part of the fun and challenge of coaching. It stimulates my skills to try and give riders fun and education in the time available, hoping that they go home feeling good about what has happened.

However, there are times that this is simply not possible because of the makeup of the combination. Turning people away is not always an option, so I have battled through lessons trying to keep people safe and make progress, while, at the same time, trying to give my full attention to others in the group. Throughout, I am wondering what I say to the rider at the end. What words of encouragement or comfort can I give and, at the same time, be honest? Do I need to get involved? Will it make any difference? It is a tricky dilemma.

My concern is, first, for the safety of the rider, and then for the welfare of the horse.

In these situations I ask myself whether it is the partnership that does not work, or the horse or the rider? Where does the blame lie? Sometimes it is neither side's fault.

Sometimes the rider is not up to the task and may never be, but there are also cases where the horse is neither trainable nor safe. These horses need professional help and have no place in the hands of an amateur rider.

All too often, I have riders return to my clinics with a horse that is unsuitable, thinking that I can help them, seeking my opinion or confirmation that "he's getting better." In the interim 12 months, the horse has cost them 10 times what they paid for it and they have had a miserable time. I ask myself, what is the point?

I can remember at one of my clinics watching a horse reluctantly jump onto a bank. And there he stood, and stood, and stood. An hour and a half later he was still there. I advised his rider that he might not be a suitable cross-country horse.

On two occasions I have advised that the horse in question should *never* be ridden again—once for a horse that went over backward twice with his rider (who was not to blame), and once for a horse that bolted dangerously (also through no fault of his rider). Neither horse had apparent reason to do what he did.

> People often need help and advice to find the right equine partner.

Sometimes, horses are just not suitable to become nice riding horses. Ex-racehorses can be a good example. I love Thoroughbreds and always have. Their extra bit of "something" appeals to me, especially for eventing. However, it is important to remember that these animals have been taught in a different way. Their life from an early, impressionable age has been to run. The aids they have learned and the life they have led is not always conducive—or easy—to change. Some ex-racehorses are retrainable and there are many stories of horses that have succeeded in other disciplines, but—and it is a very big but—this has been achieved through skilled training and careful, knowledgeable handling. This is often a professional's task. Even the quiet, easy Thoroughbred off the track will still have all the training issues associated with a young horse, with the added complication of having to retrain the conditioned reflexes that he brings with it.

People often need help and advice to find the right equine partner, preferably from someone who knows the individuals and what they need in a horse.

How to Avoid an Inappropriate Partner

These are the questions for riders to ask themselves:

➤ How good a rider are you? It is important to be critically analytical. This is difficult to do, but necessary.

➤ How much time and what facilities do you have?

➤ What do you want the horse for?

➤ If he is cheap, why? Beware!

➤ What breed of horse will suit your needs?

➤ Is size important?

➤ Age versus suitability: which is more important?

➤ Body versus mind: be aware of the beautiful-looking but unforgiving horse.

What to do with an inappropriate partner:

➤ Get a quick divorce—do not prolong the agony. Keeping an unsuitable horse will only cost money and cause heartache. Remember, riding is supposed to be pleasurable and there are other horses out there.

➤ The best way to get out is to consult people in the trade. Coaches and local dealers are good starting points.

➤ When the horse is dangerous do not discount euthanasia. It may be a kindness in the long term. If a horse is not to be ridden again, I believe we have a "responsibility of care" for that animal, as we do for other animals, like cats and dogs. I do not think that it is ethical to abdicate our responsibility by not making the right decision. I have heard of horses being let loose in the wild to fend for themselves, and horses being left in one of the less discerning homes for retired horses, waiting to die. We have a moral obligation to do the right thing by the animals that we are responsible for.

Be prepared for some blunt advice and use it constructively. It is pertinent to remember that the horse has little choice in his partner. He can't say no to you.

Sometimes it is painful for me to watch and not be able to do anything except applaud a horse's good nature and generosity. There are welfare issues that concern me and, at times, people need these pointed out to them so they can take responsibility and address them. Remember, the horse has no say.

Breaking a Vicious Circle

A vicious circle: *A sequence of reciprocal cause and effect in which two or more elements intensify and aggravate each other, leading inexorably to a worsening of the situation.*

As a coach I am presented with this teaching scenario all the time. I have to make choices, which then lead to decisions about where I start to try to break the "vicious circle." This can happen at all levels: from the international rider who sits to one side and unbalances the horse, to the novice rider who loses balance and pulls the horse in the mouth, which causes him to stop at the jump.

Sometimes it is difficult to decide just where to begin the repair process without spoiling what might be "good enough." The performance may deteriorate by dismantling things just to rebuild them, sometimes to the point that it may have been best to not bring them up in the first place. The act of rebuilding can be a long road and may not even be possible. There have been many occasions when I have chosen to leave something well alone, knowing that the rider is not well placed enough to work on the rebuild. Rebuilding requires determination.

Competition riders will often say, "I've reached this far, so why should I change?" It doesn't always help to point out how much better it could be.

Coaches are often taught that fixing the rider will make the horse go better, but I often take a different approach and choose to work on the horse. This allows me to use the rider's ability, at whatever her level, to encourage the horse to go better, and then develop the rider's feel of what *better* actually is. Horses that go better—more forward, straighter, and more regular—become easier to sit on and easier to ride. Then it becomes more straightforward to make adjustments to the rider.

Most novice riders have balance issues that make communication difficult and this, in turn, can irritate the horse. The horse then ignores the rider or becomes frustrated. This is not a criticism, merely an observation. But by working on the balance, making the rider's aids consistent and then making them more effective, things can start to look better.

Sometimes it is difficult to decide just where to begin the repair process without spoiling what might be "good enough."

More experienced riders tend to have an ingrained way of going that serves them well and is very effective. Their faults are often harder to correct because they feel that by changing they may lose their effectiveness. This becomes hard to accept, so change is less likely to happen. With any correction there has to be a desire to *want* to change. It has to be in everyone's interest to make the effort, so there has to be something in it for both horse and rider. Horses get a pat and the possibility of a better ride, while riders can achieve better results and the possibility of an easier horse to sit on.

Whichever way we decide to try and break the vicious circle, there must be a way to follow it through that the rider understands, otherwise regression is likely and things may end up worse than they were before.

CHAPTER SEVEN

Early Training

There is much you can learn about communicating with horses by study-ing the natural interaction between them. I remember once watching one of my mares teaching her foal the difference between right and wrong, do and don't, yes and no. Like everything she did, she was very clear. To begin with she made a facial expression at her foal. When that didn't work, she stamped her front foot. When that didn't work she swung her quarters toward him. Then, she would stamp her hind legs and finally she would kick him—just hard enough to get the message across.

I watched this time and time again. She was a great teacher. After the initial lessons, all she had to do was look at her foal and he got the message. She had taught him that when she asked quietly she expected an answer.

This was a good lesson for me as it taught me a method that was familiar to the horse. Ask quietly, but be prepared to up the intensity of the question until an answer is delivered. Then, just as my mare did, offer a reward. This is important because the horse needs to know he has done well to understand the process.

> The aids are like language is between two people—they have a vocabulary and an order.

The Aids

We all know that the aids are the means of communication between rider and horse. The aids are the legs, hands, weight, voice, and seat. There are also the artificial aids: the stick and spurs, and, some might also say, the martingale.

The aids are like language is between two people. They have a vocabulary, an order—a start, middle, and an end of meaning, much like any conversation. The first important point to make, however, is that the two participants must both understand the language—a *shared understanding*. They must be able to use it on the same level and know the vocabulary appropriate to the conversation.

As a raw trainee at the Talland School of Equitation in Gloucestershire, England, I was asked to ride a Grand Prix dressage horse. He was an old horse used in the school to teach people like me. In my positive way I asked him with good, clear leg aids to go forward into trot. This produced piaffe. Once he'd started I couldn't stop him! It was very good of him to offer it, but it was not what I thought I'd asked for. Clearly I was wrong!

Over the next six months this horse taught me so much about the vocabulary and subtlety needed in the use of the aids. When I watch children talk to each other, they carry on a meaningful conversation but with a limited vocabulary, often using their own words. As a human, you learn words and their meaning; you learn the structure of sentences and how to use these to converse with others. There is no difference in how you study communicating with horses.

Most horses are willing to please and want to understand, so you need a plan to guide this willingness in your direction. You need a method of reward and correction, a way of layering extras onto a simple beginning. The vocabulary you use must be logical and consistent, but it must also follow on from what has been taught before.

I liken my aids to the way I use my voice. I do not want to shout at people, I want to make myself understood with a quiet voice. It is the same with the aids. To encourage the horse to listen to and understand light aids we must avoid "shouting."

Let me outline the aids in more detail:

The Legs

The leg, the primary aid, which should come first in all communication with the horse, is a conversation starter. There are two sets of leg aids: forward riding and sideways moving. Forward aids are on the girth and sideways are behind the girth.

We begin with the young horse, or the reeducation of an older horse, by asking him to go forward with the leg on the girth and a light contact on the reins. Forward is a state of mind, so with little encouragement the horse should comply (fig. 7.1).

Then you can layer on more information. You might want the horse to be quicker in his response, but you must understand the pitfalls that could await you—beware of using more leg in any situation. Getting more from the leg doesn't mean using *more* leg. Instead, you should continue to use a light leg, but tap with the schooling whip to indicate that a quicker response is required. The leg aids have their own vocabulary: they can whisper, nudge, shout, work as a pair, or work individually. Their use must be dynamic to retain a light and quick response.

In teaching this way you retain the use of light leg aids—a "quiet voice"—to achieve an answer. This allows you to retain an ease of communication that will be vital as the horse improves his vocabulary.

The same process applies when you want to apply the sideways-moving aid. The leg is positioned slightly behind the girth to ask the horse to move over.

7.1 Whatever you are riding, remember the connection from your legs to the engine behind you.

The Hands

Much is said and written about the part the hands play in communicating with the horse. For me, it relates to what type of contact the rider wants to have. Think about being greeted with a handshake. Most of us feel comfortable with a handshake that is firm; one that gives confidence and security. This is far preferable to the limp, clammy sort that makes us recoil, or the knuckle-cruncher that leaves us with a sore hand for days.

I think the horse also likes a secure, confident contact, given by the rein aid. This is in no way a contradiction to the soft and light contact, which is often talked about. The secure, confident contact can be just as feeling and responsive, but having the horse on the end of the rein is important because then the rider knows, through feel, where he is—not only in his body but also in his mind. Too soft and light a contact often indicates unwillingness, avoidance, or shyness. A horse that offers no contact is often one of the hardest to ride as you are never quite sure where he is.

You shouldn't misinterpret a quiet hand for being an unfeeling contact. Busy hands make busy mouths. Hands that are always doing something can become an irritation to the horse and lead to bad results. The mind and mouth also become busy, so the horse drops behind the contact to avoid the busyness, or becomes numb to the bit to avoid the same feeling. From a horse's point of view, how much nicer it is when the contact is quiet!

The hands and rein aids should be there to guide and direct what the leg aids create. There is an integral link between the conversation they have with each other and the combined conversation with the horse.

The Rider's Weight

Weight and balance are closely linked. The rider's weight has to be in balance for it to be carried efficiently by the horse and for the rider to be able to communicate with subtlety.

Like any sport, the influence of the athlete's weight is a line of communication with her equipment, whether this is a tennis racket, golf club, surfboard, or a horse. The better the balance, the better the use of the weight.

The more educated the horse and rider become to the influence of weight, the more this is evidence of good schooling. Poor distribution of the rider's weight makes it difficult for the horse to carry himself. Teaching it too soon may have no effect as neither horse nor rider understands the vocabulary being used. It is part of the layering of information: the extension of vocabulary and subtlety of the aids that evolve with progressive training. Riders and coaches must appreciate this process.

The Voice

From the earliest contact with the horse, the voice is an important means of communication. From trail riding to the highest level of equestrianism, the horse responds to what he hears. You have a huge range of tone that becomes understood by the horse, so you can use your voice to convey your mood, desires, pleasure, disapproval, and encouragement.

The Seat

This is one of the aids talked about long before it is either needed or even understood by horse or rider. It becomes valuable as the education of both progresses, but talking about it too soon is a distraction and should be avoided.

The seat has many functions in improving your communication with the horse—sitting to rebalance, passively sitting in harmony, sitting to engage, or sitting to drive—but they must be used at the right time and for the right effect. Incorrect use and timing of the seat aid can be detrimental to the horse's way of going.

To sit correctly requires ability on your part (fig. 7.2). Sitting well enhances the horse's ability to move and use himself. Your pelvis must rock in time with

7.2 This rider is sitting in very good balance, which is helping her horse carry himself correctly.

the horse's back, thereby absorbing the motion and becoming at one with the movement. Some riders find this easier than others. The walk and canter are good gaits to "feel" this movement. Some riders will need to think about it and make it happen long before it happens naturally.

Sitting to the trot can be a chore, but if you spend time explaining it to your body and developing the neurological pathways that allow your pelvis to move in time with the horse's back, it is worth the effort. For those who find the sitting trot difficult (and many do), it is worth remembering that the neurological pathways have evolved to fight against pelvic movement and so make it an uncomfortable feeling for both horse and rider.

I remember well the process of teaching my body to move in time with the horse. Often, it was painful. It needed constant practice and any long spell without its use meant a period of "rehabilitation." The canter is an easier gait to sit to because the horse moves in a way that does not throw the rider out of the saddle.

Playing Games

Having talked about the aids and how they can be used as a means of communication, you know that, in reality, you may inherit, buy, or just end up with a horse that doesn't listen or understand in the conventional way. It then becomes your mission to make it better. Every horse is likely to be different on the uptake.

Playing with the horse's understanding of the aids should be methodically undertaken. Being able to use the aids effectively and independently of one another requires:

1 Knowing what you want from their use.

2 Knowing that when you use them you will get a reaction.

There may be hidden or unexpected turns along the way, but if you have a plan and the necessary skills to carry it out, then at least you can recover focus.

Horses are seldom symmetrical, so the response to the right may be different to the left. Most horses will favor one side—later, this will be seen in half-pass and shoulder-in—so the more this favor can be eliminated in the early stages, the better.

This "playing" with the horse is part of the learning process. It allows the rider to build an understanding of how to communicate. Correcting an older horse can be a slow process because erasing something that has become a bad habit takes many repetitions of the good response. I was once told that it took 3,500 good repetitions to erase one bad one—how much truth there is in this I'm not sure, but it illustrates the challenge!

> **You must be slow and methodical in doing the simple things well.**

You must be slow and methodical in doing the simple things well. To help develop this independence, you should try it to see what happens. It doesn't matter whether the horse is young, being retrained, or is more established, testing and explaining the use of the aids that can and will be used independently of each other is extremely important. Teaching any new movement should be seen as a functional exercise to begin with. You are testing to see if the aids are understood and are having the desired effect. When you and your horse both understand them, it is possible to layer on more finesse and information.

The very first time a horse is asked to move sideways is a good example. Your inside leg offers the horse to the outside leg, which receives the horse and asks him forward. This simple request must be understood before anything else can be added on. It begins the process of connection, ensuring forwardness and an independence of the aid.

Any resulting improvement in the quality of the pace is part of the layering. As the horse understands the exercise, so his coordination in how he moves his feet, controls his balance, remains light to the aid, and still produces more power, improves. This can also give the appearance of suppleness through a better understanding of the aid.

Exercises must be kept interesting, so the horse sees that there is a purpose. This is part of the *buying-in* process.

Games to Try

Exercise 1: Look, Don't Go

7.3 By asking the horse to look in one direction but stay on a line, the rider is teaching the horse that her inside leg can mean "stay straight."

The first exercise in my toolbox encourages the horse to follow a lead rein, and it is the place I like to start (fig. 7.3). I always encourage a horse to seek and follow the rein, even if in the beginning it is to find food as a reward. This simple exercise begins the skill of your inside leg being able to "hold" and influence the horse's shoulder, and the inside rein influencing the horse's "look." This is a skill that is important in every riding discipline.

- In halt, open one rein at a time. You are asking the horse to look in a direction, but his head must not be forced. The rein should be an open, offering, and positive aid, not a backward or negative one.

- Repeat with the other rein to feel whether the horse reacts evenly on both sides. His reaction should be logged for future work.

- Next, try the same thing in walk. Now, you need a way of ensuring the horse does not go in the direction the reins are offering. This doesn't mean going to the outside rein, however tempting, but means using your inside leg on the girth. To help make the request clear to the horse, position him beside a fence. He will be reluctant to bang his head or walk into the solid barrier, so he will move in the direction the inside leg is asking. Now, you begin the simple understanding that two aids can appear contradictory, but are not and need to be listened to. All sorts of props can be used to confirm this message, but it is worth taking the time to make it work as it is one of the most important messages of a horse's career.

- The outside leg also has a function, which is to look after the hindquarters. The outside rein can help, but it should not be used too much as other problems may occur.

- Work in both directions to try to make the horse as symmetrical as possible.

Adding Layers

These aids form the basis for additions to later on, when you will ask the horse for lots of different turns, movements, and positions. As the understanding of the aids being applied independently of each other develops, there is a need to add on some more information.

Now you can introduce sideways.

The inside leg just behind the girth becomes a sideways aid. When it is used with the outside rein, which controls forward movement, the horse gets the message that he has to move forward *and* sideways.

Turn-*about*-the-forehand (done from walk), leg-yielding, and the turn-on-the-haunches (also known as demi-pirouette) are good exercises to begin with. I am not a fan of turn-*on*-the-forehand, which is done from halt, as a good halt is not always easy to achieve at the beginning: it is seldom square, forward in mind, secure on the aids, secure to the contact, and up through the back, so it becomes a bad beginning from which to try and achieve something good. But when it becomes a turn-*about*-the-forehand done from walk, problems are less likely to occur.

Let's look in more detail.

Exercise 2: Turn-*About*-the-Forehand, from Walk

This is a forward-and-sideways movement with a slight bend in the direction of travel (fig. 7.4). Done from walk, the rhythm is four-time. The horse moves

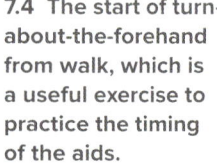

7.4 The start of turn-about-the-forehand from walk, which is a useful exercise to practice the timing of the aids.

his hindquarters around his forehand, maintaining a slight bend and staying regular in the footfalls.

➤ Your inside leg is slightly behind the girth to ask for the sideways movement, while your inside rein asks for the bend. Your outside leg is on the girth to receive the horse and ensure forwardness.

➤ Your outside rein controls the amount of bend and the forward motion.

Exercise 3: Leg-Yielding

Leg-yielding has many benefits. It is a forward-and-sideways movement—as much forward as sideways—with the horse perfectly straight and an imperceptible bend away from the direction of movement at the poll (figs. 7.5 A & B).

➤ The two most common ways to ride a leg-yield are from one line to another line (fig. 7.6) or on a circle.

➤ Your inside leg becomes the sideways aid, and the outside leg, the receiving and forward aid. Your inside rein asks for a slight bend, while the outside rein controls the amount of bend and the forwardness.

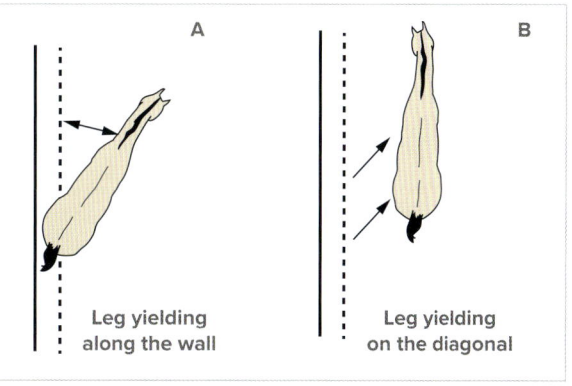

7.5 A & B The leg-yield can be ridden in different places and on varying lines.

7.6 This rider is using a fence to help her ride a leg-yield down a line.

7.7 When riding a leg-yield from line to line, you need to ask for a slight bend opposite to that of the direction of travel.

➤ To ride leg-yield from line to line often requires you to ask the horse for a bend opposite to that of the direction of travel (fig. 7.7). This is often forgotten about, so the movement is incorrect.

➤ When riding leg-yield out of a circle, it is easy to let the horse fall out through his shoulder—a bad fault that will appear in other exercises, such as shoulder-in. You need to imagine *concentric circles,* not tangent lines. The idea is to move from circle to circle while still going forward around each circle (figs. 7.8 A & B).

➤ Using "props" to help can focus your and your horse's minds (fig. 7.9).

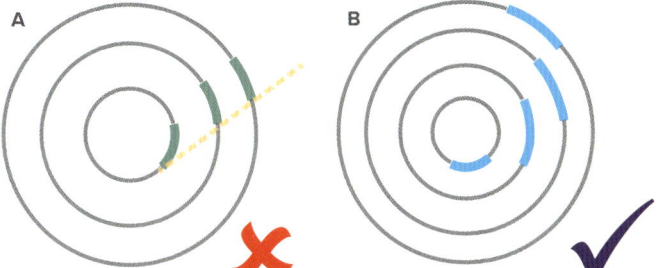

7.8 A & B Leg-yielding on a tangent line encourages a horse to fall out through the shoulder, losing straightness (A). Leg-yielding from one circle to another while moving around a series of concentric circles improves straightness, balance, independence, and understanding of the rider's aids.

7.9 Using natural props, such as this fallen log, to your advantage can help focus the horse's mind.

Exercise 4: Turn-on-the-Haunches

I like the turn-on-the-haunches, or demi-pirouette as it is known in FEI (Fédération Equestre Internationale) dressage, but as a dressage judge and coach I seldom see it ridden well. Riders generally dislike it because they don't know how to teach it to the horse or what it should look or feel like. The turn-on-the-haunches is layer upon layer of simple messages, each separated so the horse and rider understand and have a chance to recover (see "The Start Point," p. 69) if things go wrong. It allows the introduction of independent aids: aids with a different inference. It requires good timing of the aids and a horse that assimilates this information and physically carries himself in the correct way. It is equally beneficial for both the young and established horse.

> The aim is for you to feel like you can influence every part of the horse. Can you ask for and maintain the bend? Does your inside leg hold and look after the forehand? Is your outside rein able to slow the horse down, yet allow the bend? Do you get a response from the hindquarters and outside of the horse when you use your outside leg?

> If the answer to all these questions is yes, then a turn-on-the-haunches can happen.

> Too often, the bend disappears, and with it the regularity of the walk. The movement should look proud, with the horse looking in the direction he's going while moving his forehand around his hindquarters without losing the correct and regular footfall.

To See if I Can

When asked why I do certain things with horses, I often answer, "To see if I can!" It now seems a very logical answer to me, but it was not always so.

Statements like, "Leg-yielding improves suppleness," and "Shoulder-in improves engagement," used to sound sensible, but not anymore.

> **There is no magic in riding a circle, only in doing a circle correctly.**

I have a large file of notes, made at the beginning of my teaching career, that contain valuable information that formed the basis of all I know now. I was blessed with some great teachers, but as time went on, I began to question the things I had previously taken as gospel. Not because I felt they were wrong, but because I wondered whether I had misinterpreted them at the time, or whether I might understand them better now. I have often returned to these notes with new understanding.

Nothing we do with horses necessarily improves anything else. There is no magic wand that improves collection, engagement, or lightens the forehand just because we position the horse in a certain way. Just because we do a movement that a book says improves something doesn't mean it will. All it does at this stage is prove that the rider can do the movement.

My old notes said that leg-yielding improves suppleness. It can, but it can also make the trot lose forwardness, regularity, straightness, and acceptance of the aid. So simply doing movements is not the answer, even when articles written by experts say otherwise!

When a movement is ridden with forwardness, swing, a good connection, and obvious signs of acceptance, then a supple horse appears.

Why do we do circles? To see if we can! There is no magic in riding a circle, only in doing a circle correctly. It only proves that the horse, who has no concept of what a circle is, understands the rider's aids. If you can perform a pace that has quality and include it in a good circle, then the added value the circle brings is improved balance.

The ability to position a horse for the required movements is not as easy as it might appear. To do them well, without resistance and with the horse's cooperation, requires patience. Often, issues later on in a horse's education have been created by a poor start. The experienced rider will know that if certain issues are not addressed early on, there will be problems with a movement later on. For example, a horse that falls through the right shoulder as a four-year-old may find the left half-pass easier than right half-pass three years on.

You must have a clear picture of what is good and how it should look before riding any movement. There are other qualities required: forwardness, an ability to readjust the balance, and a further understanding of what comes next. It is important to know the stages taken to achieve the outcome; to look at the picture on the front of the jigsaw puzzle box before starting to put the pieces together.

When playing with young horses, it is fun to start the process of positioning. This is knowing what a movement looks like and seeing if you are able to explain to the horse the shape he needs to be in. Leg-yielding is different than shoulder-in. You need to ask yourself whether you are able to position the horse in these two different ways so that he understands what is required of him. It is a serious but fun game to play. Do it right and marks of "8" and better can be available later on; do it wrong and "7" may be the maximum available (see more about dressage marks in "Self-Assessment" on p. 72). A head tilt, a resistance, a misunderstanding is all it takes for a lesson to be flawed.

Relating Subjects

All sorts of subjects are related when training horses—movements and stages that follow directly on from what has been achieved before. So often, though, this relationship is not picked up by either the coach or the rider. This inhibits progress and can cause the horse confusion. Knowing these relationships exist allows rider and coach to layer subject upon subject and follow the training through in a progressive manner that is clear to all parties.

Let us look at some of the more common relationships and crucial links.

Relaxation...and...a Good Free Walk on a Long Rein

The crucial link: I am often asked to help people with their horse's free walk. "My horse won't stretch down," they say. "Why should he?" I ask. "Why do you want him to stretch down?"

There is a common belief that horses must stretch and relax before doing any work, but why should the horse know this?

If you always work the horse through and encourage him to look for and seek the contact, connecting him from the hind legs to the contact in front, this will become the norm for him. Encourage a state of mind of forwardness and then work him. Once the horse has worked, offer him a little longer rein. If he has been working well, he will want to relax and rest his muscles, so he will seek the contact and take the rein. This is proof of good work—this is what the free walk on a long rein movement in a dressage test is examining.

Straightness...and...Riding a Centerline

The crucial link: If a horse wobbles on the centerline, the question coaches and riders should ask is: "Why do you ride a centerline?" The answer, as I have already alluded to, is, "To see if I can."

The centerline is the test—it is what riders are being examined on. If you have proved the horse is forward and accepting your aids, then you can hold a line. This relationship goes much further than dressage. When the horse is straight, you can also ride the lines the show jumping course designer asks, and the narrow or the corner fence on the cross-country.

Trotting Poles...and...Jumping

The crucial link: Trotting poles encourage the horse to be more active, so if the rider applies her leg aids at the same time, the horse will associate this with lifting his legs. This can be used on takeoff. Apply a light leg aid—the same as if you are negotiating a pole—and the horse is likely to respond with a better jump. This is because from the horse's perspective the neurological pathways are very similar.

The Turn-on-the-Haunches...and...Half-Pass in Walk

The crucial link: The turn-on-the-haunches and the half-pass require the same aid from you and the same shape from the horse. The only difference is that in the turn-on-the-haunches your outside rein aid restricts forward movement and the horse moves around the hind-quarters, while in the half-pass, the outside rein allows the forward movement in the desired direction (fig. 7.10).

Riding Circles...and...Riding Show Jumping and Cross-Country Courses

The crucial link: All course designers use circles and half-circles as a basis for the approach and for the positioning of fences, so being able to ride accurate circles and half-circles of all shapes and sizes means you are reproducing the skills used in one discipline and transferring them directly to another (fig. 7.11).

How Much Should We Ask?

As we relate subjects we must be careful not to hurry the link. A period of consolidation should always follow the introduction of something new. Allow time for the horse and rider to become secure in the understanding before asking for the next piece of the jigsaw in question. You must be aware of asking too

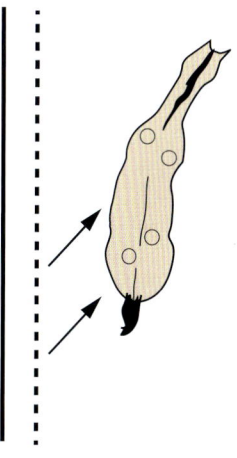

7.10 The positioning of the horse at the start of a half-pass.

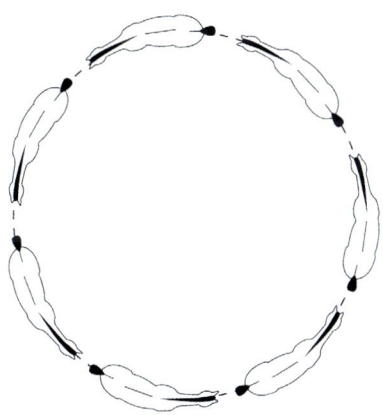

7.11 Being able to ride an accurate circle is vital whatever your discipline.

much, too soon, and accepting an incorrect response simply because everyone wants to move on. This will often be difficult to correct and have repercussions later.

> ➤ Asking too soon: The horse will often offer sideways in preference to forward and straight. It can then be difficult to reinstate *forward*.

> ➤ Asking too much: The horse will put up a resistance physically and mentally at the point he finds things difficult. He will shorten his step, tighten through the back, and stop going forward willingly. This resistance point can sometimes be difficult to overcome later on as it remains in his subconscious. Better it isn't there at all.

> ➤ Accepting incorrect: When you are presented with a good answer you should willingly accept it, rejoice, and try it again to see if it was luck or proper understanding. If, however, you are presented with a "nearly" good answer, you need to be quick and clear with your response. What should you do? Should you ask again and only accept a good answer? Or is "nearly good" good enough? This is not an easy question to answer, but generally when I feel the horse is trying to please and find the correct answer, I will probably accept it. If, however, I feel he is plucking any old answer out of the hat and not buying into the thought process, then I try again for something better. Often, the horse's character is a deciding factor. We do not always make the correct choice.

All sorts of subjects are related when training horses—movements and stages that follow directly on from what has been achieved before.

The same applies when a coach interacts with a pupil. Putting "good" and "correct" in people's minds is a good thing for their understanding as they strive for better. How much should a coach push or nudge? So much is down to the individual receiving the push and nudge, and this can only be judged by the coach and how he views the relationship.

CHAPTER EIGHT

Developing Skills

Throughout the process of progressive training, you are layering more information onto a secure platform. In doing this, you are building on something dependable, ever present, and reliable. As there are so many different building processes going on at the same time there are many secure platforms being created. Often these are at different levels and stages, but they have become part of the process that provides a dependable "return point" when things go a little wobbly or wrong. These are what I call "start points."

The Start Point

A "start point" is a moment or a stage in training when things work well—not once, but consistently so. It is a place you can visit and know the result will be the same every time—a "go-to" spot where you can explain things to the horse. It is often the moment an aid is understood, which allows you to move on and explain the next step. It is a springboard for something new.

With the young horse, the start point can be the feeling of him "taking you" forward. This willingness to go allows you to add on an explanation of straightness and then regularity. When straightness or regularity is lost, it is important to quickly return to the start point—forwardness.

A coach uses a start point to clarify things to the rider, the horse, or both. So being aware of the start point stops you from going off course. By going back and confirming a moment that is right and understood by all, you can

Being aware of the start point stops you from going off course.

keep sight of the correct path ahead. It is too easy to get drawn along a side road thinking it will be all right in the end because it seldom is!

Even well-educated partnerships need a start point—a place that can be revisited to reconfirm the good things, which can easily get lost as the tasks become harder. Counter-canter is a good example. Introduced too soon and the horse quickly learns to change canter leads, to the point that a mere whisper of counter-canter and he switches. You must spend a great deal of time at the previous start point—riding a variety of shapes in true canter—to teach the horse that he must keep paying attention to your aid.

A start point is equally important when jumping. Riders often try too hard to get things right and in doing so it all goes wrong! My advice in this instance is to have a start point of cantering to a small fence thinking only of the quality of the canter. By doing this simple thing well, it reminds you of the qualities that can then be taken into more demanding tasks.

I am continually reminding myself and my pupils of cross-country start points (see p. 69). There is a tendency while going cross-country to start over-riding and taking over from the horse. There are all sorts of gremlins trying to convince you there is a better way of doing things, which leads you to forget to keep doing the simple things that you are trained to do. There will always be a jump on the course you can use to safely remind the horse of the ownership priorities of *pace* and *line* (see p. 24), and *jump*. This may be a straightforward jump where you allow the horse to make his own decisions to ensure he is not dependent on you. This is the start point that should be established in the warm-up arena, so on course the rider is merely confirming that it is still working.

Layering to Elevate Performance

When I watch the dressage phase at any top-level event, it is interesting to see how the judging works out in real terms. Usually, the field is divided into two groups: those who can do "good" work (for a mark of "7" or more) and those who

The Start Point Is:

➤ A tool for horses and riders to use to regroup.

➤ A coaching tool to reestablish the horse and rider's comfort zone.

➤ A springboard for a move to the next level.

can do "satisfactory" work (for a mark of "6" or less). The riders all know where they are going and the picture they are aiming to create, and they are doing their best. So what makes the difference?

It is not always clear to the observers whether the performance they are watching is on a good or a bad day, but there is usually reason to say, "That could be so much better if...." In some instances there is something fundamental that needs addressing before any improvement can happen, but often the "if" is simply a thin layer on top of what the horse and rider are already showing.

Satisfactory work is functional; good work has an added extra on top. Often, we try to produce good when we cannot produce functional. It may be that the "7s" group understood and demonstrated "through with impulsion," while the "6s" group did not. This is an instance of layering. The "7s" group had layered work onto the basics: the accuracy of the transitions, the acceptance of the aids through these transitions, the rideability of the horse through each movement, and so on. They had in place a solid start point.

The moving-on process required to raise a performance to the next level is sometimes challenging for the horse. Until this point, the rider has been telling him that what he is doing has been acceptable, but now he needs convincing that more is wanted! Some horses are happy to oblige, others less so.

> **Often, we try to produce good when we cannot produce functional.**

The example of "through with impulsion" is a good one to follow. "Through" means there is no resistance between the leg, hindquarters, back, poll, jaw, bit, and hand. This is how you would like every horse to work because when this happens the horse is "available" to you.

For higher marks, you need to find more available energy in order to improve the paces and way of going.

How do you do this?

Trot poles can be helpful because the trot becomes livelier as you use them, and this automatically opens the door of the horse's mind to the feeling of more energy. The tricky part is to recreate that feeling when the poles are taken away. As the poles bring openness and life to the trot, you should apply the leg aid in time with the stride to make the link in the horse's mind and tell him that this is something extra to normal. Quiet repetition reinforces the idea, and it does not take long before the horse begins to offer something more.

This is the beginning of impulsion or "available energy" and you can now layer this on to the functional trot or canter and begin to demonstrate a pace that is worth more than a "6." It becomes easier to layer better on top of "satisfactory" when the basics are secure. Being able to produce this satisfactory work then becomes a good start point.

Another way to layer on a little extra is to work on increasing and decreasing the pace. To elevate a working pace to the next level work on the two ends of the scale—bigger and smaller. By focusing on maintaining the constant qualities of *forward, straight,* and *regular,* it is possible to improve the working pace simply through enhancing the understanding of what the aids are asking, and working toward a more adjustable step with a greater availability of energy.

Self-Assessment

As a rider I used to ask myself, "What mark would I give for this work?"

To answer it constructively I needed to know the marks that relate to the words in a dressage test:

"0" = **Not performed**	"6" = **Satisfactory**
"1" = **Very bad**	"7" = **Fairly good**
"2" = **Bad**	"8" = **Good**
"3" = **Fairly bad**	"9" = **Very good**
"4" = **Insufficient**	"10" = **Excellent**
"5" = **Sufficient**	

I ask myself: "Why was that worth a '7,' but not an '8'?" In answering this question I need to be honest. Not being honest will not help me improve. Then I ask myself what I need to do to make up the difference. How do I achieve a better result? This is a dynamic answer that always changes. The first half of a circle might be worth a "7," but the second half, an "8." The transition into the pace might only be good enough for a "6.5," but the pace itself worth an "8." This becomes a process that keeps the mind busy and the body active solving problems and making things better. Having a continual Q & A encourages a mindset of self-assessment and continues to develop the all-important "feel."

Describing "feel" is something I have struggled with for years. The best and most succinct answer I have come up with is, "doing the right thing at the right time." Others simply call it "awareness." The more experienced the rider, the quicker she is able to respond to what is happening underneath her. Should she keep doing what she is doing or recover what she might have lost and make it better again? This is "feel."

Coaches should use this method to encourage riders to become more self-sufficient and less dependent. I try to become dispensable when I teach, and I believe the aim of all coaches should be to encourage riders to be responsible and think for themselves. Riders do not have the luxury of being coached while actually competing, so it is necessary for them to stand on their own feet, make decisions, and then see that they happen.

> **Feel is doing the right thing at the right time.**

"What are you trying to do?" This is a challenging question, asked in many ways for many different reasons. What is more, where the emphasis is placed changes the meaning:

> *What* are you trying to do?
> What *are* you trying to do?
> What are *you* trying to do?
> What are you *trying* to do?

It makes people stop and think. "What am I trying to do? Do I have any idea? Do I have a plan or am I only doing what I've been told to do?"

When using a challenging question or statement, the coach has to be aware of the reaction it provokes. Most people do not like being challenged as they find it an affront or a criticism. Sometimes it produces a combative reaction; sometimes it prompts a doubting reaction. Either way, it is important to get a reaction.

The follow-up is critical and the moment must not be lost. A coach's foot is now in the door; it is time to "sell one's wares," time to open a dialogue and explore thoughts and ideas. As riders search for an answer, they tend to gather thoughts in three predictable ways:

1 The "sound-bite" reaction: The rider offers impressive-sounding sentences, words, or statements that she has been taught, heard, or read.

2 The more detailed explanation: The rider justifies her reasons for what she is doing in a complicated way.

3 The exasperated response: The rider gives up the challenge of an intellectual debate.

Coaches should engage in the debate without being the "know it all" and the "I know better" type of person. By keeping the dialogue open and exploring the pupil's understanding while feeding in his or her own ideas, it is possible to take people on a journey: by opening a new understanding of words and expressions; changing old, possibly misunderstood thoughts; and helping clarify existing ideas.

As riders rearrange their thoughts it is important for the coach's explanations to be clear and logical. Riders need to at least understand, even if they are yet to be convinced. Practical demonstration of a theory can then confirm the validity of the process: to see, hear, and ultimately do.

> It is important for coaches to make riders aware that all the time they should be thinking.

This self-assessment is equally important when jumping. As a rider, I was always asking myself whether the canter was good enough, if not why not, and what needed doing to correct it.

Now, when I'm coaching, and I see some nice work, I try to make the rider aware of it. I don't say, "That looks good" in a conversational way—although that can be important—but I ask the rider directly and immediately, "How does that feel?" or "What did you do to get that trot/canter?" The responsibility is now passed to the rider, who can feel, assess, and repeat.

It is important for coaches to get into the habit of questioning and make riders aware that all the time they should be thinking:

"6" = Satisfactory = correct but lacking something = the challenge to improve

and

Marks = the right words = riding qualities = the challenge to improve

When this becomes second nature there is an improvement in all parties' jobs and the way they work together. Coach and rider begin to think as one and find solutions. In turn, this makes the rider more self-sufficient and independent of the coach. Thinking the same thing is a huge confidence boost for the rider because it becomes an endorsement of what she is doing.

My Scales of Training

The expression Scales of Training (also called the Training Scale or Training Pyramid) is one of the most used in some areas of riding. I say "some" because many participants in the modern disciplines have never heard of them, or have no interest in their use, yet their horses can still be happy and well-schooled.

The Scales of Training incorporate six or seven qualities (depending on which textbook you read) that are deemed necessary to put together in order to produce a "well-schooled" horse. Each quality has a dependence on the others and they are all developed in a progressive manner. This way of training is sometimes called the "classical" method; however, given that the words and qualities have evolved from the German method of training

A Story About Headsets

At an international event I was attending, I watched a friend's horse warming up for dressage and was impressed with how well he was going. I saw the trainer talking into her microphone in an intent way, obviously concentrating hard on what was going on, so I went across to the other side of the arena to talk to the owner. I remarked how well I thought the horse and rider were doing. She said. "I know. I hate to tell the trainer that I have the rider's earphone in my pocket!"

The moral of this story is that the rider felt perfectly comfortable on her own doing what she had learned—and was able to do it without any outside help! Time to let go.

only in the last 50 years, "classical" is hardly an appropriate term.

When I am told, "I train my horse using the Classical Method," or "I use the Training Scale when schooling," or even "I train my horse the natural way," I am always wary. It only takes a scratch of the surface to discover how little is really understood. It appears to me that so often riders and coaches talk about the use of the Training Scale as a validation for their work while carrying on with simple Progressive Training, or they simply misunderstand what the Training Scale means.

When you are asking your horse to do something, you should understand it yourself.

When I ask riders to explain what they are doing, their replies are very revealing. People often find it difficult to put into words or explain what they are trying to achieve, but when it is something they are asking their horse to do, I feel strongly that they should understand it themselves. It is only fair to the horse.

Let us look deeper, starting with the qualities that commonly make up my Training Scale. I always include *forwardness* in my Scale—bizarrely, it is a quality that does not appear in other books, yet we all know that it is the single most important starting point. Without forwardness, nothing else happens. To assume it is there at all or that it remains is foolish.

Forwardness

This is the feeling of the horse *taking* the rider. It is a state of mind and a prerequisite to everything in riding.

Rhythm

If you think of rhythm purely as the footfall, it is either correct or incorrect, and the correct footfall must be *"regular."* Both words stand by themselves and should not be lumped together.

Tempo also comes under this heading. This is the speed of the rhythm. It, too, stands by itself and is an important quality to understand.

Relaxation

This is the horse being comfortable with the process, what is being asked of him, and his understanding your aids. It is not dependent on his head and neck being in a low frame.

Suppleness

"Stiffness" is thought of as a physical issue and not as it should be, which is a resistance to the rider's aids. Suppleness is also perceived as being something physical, when suppleness is, in fact, the appearance of a horse truly accepting—and understanding—your aids. Suppleness is, therefore, a mental acceptance that allows for a certain physical appearance.

Contact

This is the mutual feel the horse has on the end of your rein. The horse must hold the bit in a non-resistant way. The lower jaw and the poll both have a role to play in this non-resistance. You must strive to be consistent with the contact so there is an appearance of harmony. To achieve this, there must be elasticity in both reins.

Connection

I like to include this quality in addition to *contact*. It is the feeling that what you are asking for with your legs has a direct link to what you receive in your hand. The horse feels connected from back to front.

Impulsion

This is the "available energy" and desire to go forward. Without a desire to *take you* forward, there is no chance of creating energy, and without energy, it is impossible to create impulsion. The horse's mind always comes before the body. An acceptance and understanding of the aid will allow you to tap into this energy, whatever it is needed for.

Straightness

This is when the horse's hind legs follow the front legs, which follow the head and neck, on whatever line you ask for. The spine is on the line of motion.

Collection

When the horse's hind legs carry more weight and there is an increase in power, the result is a lightening of the forehand.

The Training Orbit

The qualities I've just discussed are often depicted as a pyramid or a ladder, with *Rhythm* at the bottom and *Collection* at the top, but this gives a false impression of how they each interact with one other. There is a belief, perpetrated by some coaches and held by riders, that says you start at the bottom and work up. This suggests that without one level or rung on the ladder being secure, it is inadvisable to move on to the next. Nothing could be further from the truth (see the sidebar "My Youngsters at Four," p. 42).

I believe there is another way to look at this subject. A way that is much more like what happens in reality.

Let us start with the horse and rider at the center of the process. Around them revolve many qualities that the partnership dips into and out of (fig. 8.1). There are times when great forwardness and impulsion is achieved, then disappears. There are times, even with the young or inexperienced horse, when collection appears and then goes. There are times when all the desired qualities appear together, and then desert you. These moments serve as an introduction to what can come later. It is important to appreciate them, enjoy

A Valuable Lesson

Mrs. Molly Sivewright was a most remarkable horsewoman. She was the matriarch of the famous Talland School of Equitation in Ampney Knowle, England, where I spent several years training. During my time there I looked after a young dressage stallion called Gussy. Mrs. Sivewright would ride Gussy in the school when we were all having a lesson, and as we all filed out at the end, she would stay and Gussy would become animated at our leaving. This produced the beginnings of passage and piaffe. It was way before he ever needed them, or was educated enough to know what they were, but they were glimpses of what he would revisit later in his training. Mrs. Sivewright often asked us all to return and leave a few more times in order that she could "complete" her lesson with Gussy.

them, and ask yourself how and why they happened, then store them away, safe in the knowledge they will reappear later. This applies whatever the horse and rider's level of experience. Grand Prix dressage horses need to dip in and out of qualities to reconfirm their availability and correctness. When the rider corrects a movement, she will more often than not return to the basics and find a start point (see p. 69). The more schooled the horse and rider, the closer the Training Orbits and the more readily available the qualities become (fig. 8.2).

The Training Spiral

The other way I like to think about this subject is a Training Spiral (fig. 8.3). Every time the partnership moves around the Spiral on their way up, each quality is visited and revisited as the horse develops physically and mentally. There will be an overlap and interaction of these qualities; many are not finite, but depend on the stage of schooling. The journey goes round and hopefully upward in a progressive way. Many of the qualities are visited often, new ones arrive, and they all evolve as their journey upward continues.

A four-year-old horse may have some impulsion or a degree of collec-

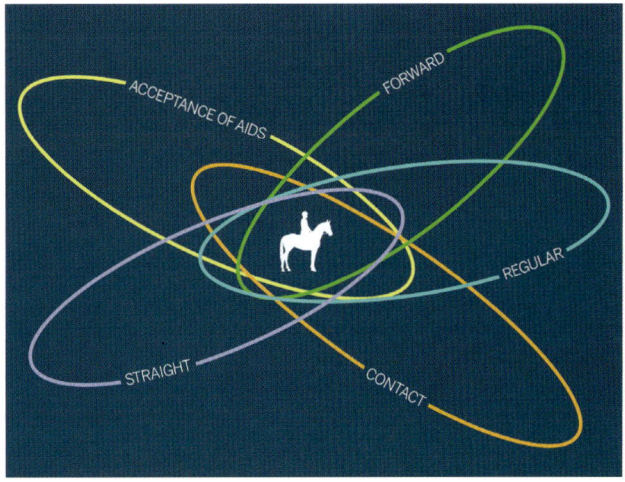

8.1 The Training Orbit has various qualities that horse and rider dip in and out of on their educational journey. These qualities may be familiar or brand new.

8.2 The Advanced Training Orbit: The more educated the partnership, the closer together and more readily available the qualities become.

FORWARD

COLLECTION

ACCEPTANCE

BALANCE

IMPULSION

REGULAR

FORWARD

STRAIGHT

BALANCE

CONTACT

RELAXATION

CONTACT

ACCEPTANCE

STRAIGHT

8.3 The Training Spiral: As horse and rider continue their education, many of the qualities are visited often, new ones arrive as the layering of information and skills becomes possible, and they all evolve as their journey upward continues.

tion, but not as much as an older or more schooled horse. It should not, therefore, be considered that one quality follows another, or that one has to be established before moving on to the next. It is a dynamic, constantly evolving process that we hope will keep progressing as horse and rider develop.

All the qualities in the Scales of Training are valid as part of a progressive way of training. The problem lies in how they are thought of and taught.

Demystifying Common Expressions

There are so many different equestrian expressions in common use. They can mean different things to different people, they can be interpreted in different ways by coaches and riders, and, occasionally, they even mean different things in different languages (fig. 8.4)! Really, though, all that matters is how they are communicated to the horse.

Here are some common examples:

Soft and Round

Two words that are often used to describe a contact and an outline, but what do they really mean? How *soft and round* do you want the horse?

Put simply: A contact is something that is there in the rider's hand. Difficulties arise when it is too light. When the horse avoids taking any feel from the

8.4 To avoid confusion, coach, rider, and horse need to find a simple, logical method of communication.

hands, it cannot be a contact! As I said earlier, I like to think of the contact as a good handshake. It should be something the horse holds with confidence, understands, and feels; something that you can reciprocate.

To be "round" is meant to describe a horse working over his back into a contact. However, being behind the contact and hiding the head too deep is not round, nor is hollowing the back—these are signs of avoidance.

Down in Front

This is when the horse's head and neck is lower than what would be a normal head carriage for that particular horse. *Down in front* is often perceived to be somewhere for the horse to be when you want him to relax or warm up. Often, though, he is simply put there because the rider thinks it is the correct place.

Put simply: You should aim for the horse to be working over his topline and seeking the contact, which you have allowed to be longer. This demonstrates correct schooling and can be used to allow the relaxation of muscles after work.

Up in Front

An expression used to refer to a thought that if the horse is ridden with his head and neck in a higher frame than normal, it will illustrate "correct" schooling, a degree of collection, and an uphill tendency.

Put simply: The horse has to be *up in front* for the right reasons. To physically try to force a horse's frame uphill is wrong. A horse's frame will naturally become more "up" when he demonstrates a change in balance. The joints of his hind limbs flex more, he takes more weight off the front end, and a degree of collection happens. This will show itself as the horse being lighter and more up in front.

Uphill

This is a good dressage term, but how can a horse be uphill when he is traveling on the flat?

Put simply: When a feeling evolves that the energy created from the horse's hind end is able to support some of the weight from his front end, the rider will feel the horse become more "up" in front of her, giving a feeling of being *uphill.*

Get a Better Rhythm

This is a misused expression. The FEI definition of *Rhythm* is: "The correct footfall of the pace." This means that the rhythm is either correct or incorrect; it is not possible to "get a better one."

Put simply: When the rhythm is correct, it is your job to keep it regular. That is the test being judged. The FEI directives state, "Rhythm and regularity." The first must be correct, while the second must be maintained.

Inside Leg to Outside Hand

This statement causes more confusion than almost any other. Perhaps because it is an expression of a "feeling," rather than something that must actively happen. It is often taught as a way of getting the horse on the bit or in riding schooling figures. So often it produces the wrong interpretation with the rider overusing the inside leg, which then creates crookedness and confusion for the horse. The issue is then compounded when the rider is jumping and is told to hold the horse with the outside rein around the corner before a jump, as this produces outside bend and causes the horse to fall in.

Put simply: When the rider rides evenly from both legs to both hands it produces a secure contact—one that the horse will relish. As the rider guides the horse in a particular direction, the inside rein becomes a little lighter. The inside leg is required to hold and define the line the horse has to stay on, creating a feeling of the horse being between the contact of the outside rein and the inside leg. Importantly, though, the horse is not driven to the outside rein, and therefore, there is no loss of straightness.

More Leg!

This is a well-used expression to encourage a horse to do more, but how and when should you apply the aid?

Put simply: You should aim to get more from the leg you are using. When coaches say, "Use more leg," it is a quick statement that takes riders down a cul-de-sac. The law of diminishing returns now applies—the more we do the less we get—as more leg will often produce less response from the horse, who becomes immune to the rider's constant pressure. To say, "Get more from the leg you are using," is cumbersome, so it is seldom used, but it is the correct expression.

> **The development of horse and rider is a dynamic, constantly evolving process.**

Steer the Horse with Your Leg

But from the beginning we are taught that we steer with the reins!

Put simply: Your legs are part of the whole package of aids used to guide the horse. When riding shoulder-in, for example, your inside leg is needed to guide the horse down a line that he is not looking down. When the shoulder-in is turned into a half-pass, your outside leg steers the horse sideways. These aids work in tandem with the reins and are a combination of all four of the independent aids.

Wrap the Horse Around the Inside Leg

Unless this statement is explained carefully, you can end up thinking that the inside leg should be actively moving and doing something. This produces the wrong result.

Put simply: Your inside leg needs to become a pillar that stops the horse falling in. While the inside rein asks the horse's head and neck to look in a particular direction—left, for example—the outside rein (in this case the right rein) allows for the desired amount of bend. Meanwhile, your outside (right) leg prevents the horse's hindquarters from swinging out. Effectively, therefore, there are three aids doing the "wrapping around," while the inside leg stays holding its position.

Use Your Seat!

This is another overused expression and one that encourages you to use your seat in an overactive way that the horse does not understand. This becomes a waste of time and effort.

Put simply: When the horse has been taught that your seat can be an additional aid to influence his way of going, it can be very helpful. Your seat can help rebalance him, it can precede a transition, create more impulsion, and help produce bigger and more powerful paces. But when neither party understands what it means, it is a pointless aid to talk about.

CHAPTER NINE

The Gaits

The horse sport industry has changed enormously in recent years. Specialized breeding has produced different traits, types, and variations on a particular model. Sometimes this breeding works, but often genetics throws wild cards into the mix and it does not.

I am often asked what I look for in an event horse, and I reply, "It's a bit like finding a wife [pause for dramatic effect]; you have to like the individual as you are going to be spending a lot of time together."

It doesn't matter whether a horse is a happy hacker or a potential competition partner, you want him to look at you with interest and a positive disposition. I cannot overemphasize the importance of the word and concept *forward*. I don't want to be pushing my horse along out on a ride, I don't want to be pushing him around a Grand Prix show jumping track, and I certainly don't want to be pushing him around Badminton. I would not employ someone who did not walk positively into work, nor would I employ someone who talked too much. For this reason, I don't like horses that lag behind or whinny constantly.

When looking at a horse as a prospective purchase, you must be clear about what you want him for. Focus on the important traits that suit the task. It makes life a lot easier, for example, if a jumper has a natural canter, so don't be distracted by a flashy trot. By the same token, natural mechanics are important for high-level dressage, and a horse built on the forehand is unlikely to progress to the top.

The skill of riding and coaching is how to develop the not-so-good to make it the best it can be.

There will always be exceptions to the rule; no horse is perfect, so there may have to be compromise. The skill of riding and coaching is how to develop the not-so-good to make it the best it can be.

A horse's trot can always be improved, but to improve the basic canter is much harder. If the trot is what is mostly required, then buy a nice trot. If the canter is important—and it will be for all jumping—look carefully at the canter.

Changing a horse's biomechanics is sometimes possible, but it is a slow process and normally a professional's job. A horse built upside-down, down-hill; a horse with his neck set low on his shoulders or feet that don't land squarely on the ground (he doesn't have to be a straight mover); or a horse with his hocks out behind him cannot be remedied.

Horses with obvious physical issues are best left well alone—you can encounter enough problems without buying them. But conformational issues need to be considered in relation to the reason for purchase. As a rule, when looking at the gaits, the horse should willingly take the handler forward with a loose, free, easygoing, and clearly defined step. To listen as well as look at the footfall is always helpful.

Is the Gait Correct?

As a rider, coach, and judge, this is the first question I ask myself. A gait that is correct has to have the correct rhythm to start with. Without having this uppermost in your mind, you might start with it being wrong—or end up with it going wrong. If the walk is lateral (see p. 88) or the canter is four-beat, then the answer is no. The trot will always be two-time (except with a "pacer," then it will be a lateral two-time), even if he is lame. When you don't start with "correct," it will influence how and what you do when you ride. As a coach, it will affect how and what I teach. Nothing that you or I do should affect the integrity of the gait. It must remain "pure."

When the horse learns something that is not correct it can be difficult to redefine it in his mind. This is why the first and subsequent lessons must teach "correct," to ensure this impression lasts the longest.

Coaches need to be clear what they are teaching and know when it is being understood.

What to Look For

The Walk

A good walk gives a comfortable ride, while a bad walk becomes a chore. You will have heard people say that it is easy to ruin a good walk, therefore, it is best left alone. I am not sure I agree. I think it is important for the horse to be comfortable with the rider communicating with him at all times. There is no reason for him to become upset so long as you are consistent and tactful with your conversation.

Walks can be improved by encouraging the horse to understand the use of the seat and legs because developing swing and a willingness to step bigger comes from the horse not running away from the aids.

What to look for:

➤ A clearly defined rhythm of four beats.

➤ Swing through the whole body.

➤ Overtrack of the footfall.

➤ A step that is trying to cover the ground and stay regular.

Common walk problems:

➤ Not forward: This is a state of mind. A horse will "go" if this is his conditioned response. The rider needs to ensure this happens.

➤ Jogging: This sometimes happens through excitement or anticipation, while at other times it is a misunderstanding of the aid. Either way, it is irritating when it happens in a dressage test! Although it feels counterintuitive, it is important for you to not take the leg off when the horse jogs as this signifies a reward for something you do not want. Instead, close the leg aids and push the horse into walk. As he walks, soften the aid by way of reward for something you want. If the horse is touchy to the leg aids, it is important to persist in a tactful way to reinforce the acceptance of the leg as a non-intimidating aid.

Turn-about-the-forehand is a useful exercise to try because any sideways movement that allows you to get your leg on and engage with the horse will help you take back control and continue the conversation (see p. 52).

➤ Lateral Walk: This is where the right legs move as a pair, the left legs do the same, and the walk becomes two-beat, or almost two-beat, rather than four-beat. It can appear when you are least expecting it, and it is difficult to work with. It tends to arrive when the walk starts to be collected. As a coach, it is important to take all the pressure off horse and rider and allow the walk to return to normal before trying again.

Turns-about-the-forehand and leg-yields can be helpful in solving this problem as both encourage the horse to listen to the aids without giving him the opportunity of going lateral.

The Trot

A flashy trot, however appealing, may not always be desired. In dressage, it may initially be marked well, but for show jumping, it has no value, and in eventing, it becomes a tease! People think it looks good, but forget that 80 percent of what most horses need to do is from canter. A beat with clarity and push from the hind legs has huge scope for developing into a good trot.

What to look for:

➤ A clearly defined, two-beat rhythm.

➤ Swing through the whole body.

➤ Overtrack of the footfall and a footfall that is light with a degree of natural balance and cadence.

Common trot problems:

➤ General note: Most problems in trot appear when you try to change the working trot to produce some of the other trots.

➤ Losing the regularity: This tends to be a result of losing balance, either through too much power that the horse has not yet learned to control, or too much speed with no power so the horse's back legs cannot catch up. It is resolved by retracing the training steps and going back to confirm the ability to connect the horse from the back to the front and to check the communication line from your leg to the horse's back legs. A willingness to take you forward will also make it easier to maintain regularity.

> **A flashy trot, however appealing, may not always be desired.**

➤ On the forehand and wide behind (in medium trot): This happens when the horse—and possibly the rider—have not taken on board the rebalance, which I discuss in the next section (see "The Rebalance" on p. 93). Impulsion becomes propulsion, which pushes the horse faster without his hind legs coming underneath him. This means that he lacks the balance to control the power.

  To help correct this, aside from practicing the rebalance, direct transitions (missing out a gait) are also really useful—particularly trot-halt-trot—as they require a quick response from the horse and a commitment from you not to let the energy run out the front door. This produces a better balance, push, and openness of step.

➤ Slowing and shortening the step and frame when asked to collect, with no change to the hind leg and no increase in power: This is a similar problem to the one above. Horse and rider need to understand that power has to come from the hind legs as a result of using the rebalance. There needs to be a conversation—possibly with a dressage whip in hand—to remind the horse what needs to happen to ensure the connection remains.

The Canter

Every discipline requires a horse with a good canter. Dressage tests include a high proportion of canter work, show jumping is done in canter, and in eventing, 80 percent of the work is carried out in this gait. But trying to improve a canter is not easy. It can be difficult for you to explain to the horse that you want more controllable power. A program of improving the impulsion and the balance will go a long way to improving the canter.

What to look for:

➤ A natural balance that allows the horse to carry himself without resorting to speed.

➤ A clearly defined rhythm of three beats with an equally clear moment of suspension between each sequence.

➤ A horse that prefers canter rather than trot when being loose schooled.

Common canter problems:

➤ General note: Almost all canter problems manifest themselves in the same way—a loss of suspension. A three-beat rhythm with a moment of suspension must always be present as this is not only an indication of the horse's natural way of going, but also how much energy is available.

➤ Loss of suspension when you rebalance in an effort to improve the collection (not a positive outcome): To avoid this, try using exercises that facilitate the horse's learning of shortening, but encourage the hind legs to keep "jumping."

Useful exercises include:

➤ Increasing and decreasing the gait.

➤ Decreasing and increasing the gait (they are not the same).

Try decreasing the gait and reducing the size of the circle, then actively increase the canter out of a smaller shape. This encourages the horse to find his own balance and become less dependent on you. The rider can continue to ask for more hind leg activity (especially when using the dressage whip in a tactful way).

➤ For a horse with a big, open canter, working on a shorter canter is helpful, but always be sure that in trying to make it better you don't lose what was good.

➤ Begin from a place where the horse is comfortable and use this as a starting point. Increasing and decreasing the gait on different sized circles is also a great way of improving the balance and availability of energy. Anticipating the increase will also encourage the horse to get his "push" ready. Note: Much can be lost in a rider's efforts to improve the canter. Horses may become tighter and show signs of tension, but if they are allowed to learn rather than us trying to teach them, fewer problems are likely to arise.

> **Every discipline requires a horse with a good canter.**

➤ Counter-canter: When used correctly, at the appropriate time and with thought, counter-canter is a good way to improve balance, straightness, and self-carriage. I caution its use because, used badly, it can cause as many issues as it improves. Asking too soon, when the horse doesn't really listen to the aids, will probably cause the horse to break back into trot and there will be little you can do about it.

To introduce the exercise, your should exaggerate the aids to ensure the horse knows he should remain in the canter he is in. Move him in the desired direction with the inside leg on the girth, but avoid too much bend or he will not remain straight. When coming back into true canter, make sure the outside leg and rein straighten the horse and keep bringing the forehand in front of the hindquarters. *Be positive* when returning to true canter to maintain the connection and forwardness.

9.1 This combination is demonstrating a good shoulder-fore, where the horse's forehand is moved slightly to the inside of the line.

9.2 A & B Here, the horse is showing shoulder-in, with more angle than in the previous photo of shoulder-fore (A). Diagram showing the three tracks of shoulder-in (B).

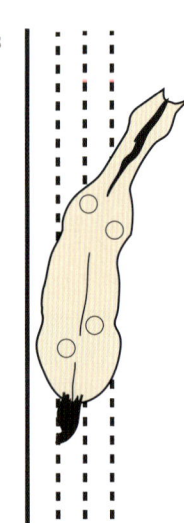

➤ Shoulder-fore: This is where the forehand is moved slightly to the inside (fig. 9.1). Any greater angle than this and the movement becomes a shoulder-in (figs. 9.2 A & B). Beware of too much bend through the neck and remember it is *shoulder*-fore, so it is the shoulder, not the neck, that is being moved to the inside. This movement benefits the canter because it brings the horse's inside hind leg more under his body, so creating the opportunity for a better balance. It also improves the horse's awareness of your aids and what they mean.

The Rebalance

The "rebalance" is one of if not *the* most important lessons taught to horse and rider. Without it, flatwork, jumping, and cross-country become devalued.

I wish that I had a dollar for every different explanation of the "half-halt" that I have heard in my years as a coach. It is not that riders are always wrong, but the logic of *why* is often not clear.

For this reason, I try to stay well away from the expression "half-halt" because it conjures up all sorts of contradictory thoughts in people's minds. I prefer "rebalance." Like a lot of horse terminology, I find that by substituting commonly used words for different ones, the meaning remains the same yet the principle is somehow easier for people to grasp and act on. The rebalance has many uses. I will add my twist on this much misunderstood, yet very vital part of riding.

To give the rebalance its full name, I call it "the rebalance within the gait." The "re" is short for "*re*assess," "*re*adjust," and "*re*think." For a horse to be in balance, his weight must be evenly distributed over all four feet. If something changes to make the rider reassess, readjust, or rethink this equilibrium, then a rebalance is needed.

> **When horses are allowed to learn rather than us trying to teach them, fewer problems are likely to arise.**

When to Use the Rebalance

➤ In preparation for a transition: It is a calling to attention where you tell the horse that something is about to happen.

➤ When you want to make a change or adjustment to the gait and ask the horse, "Are you listening to my request?"

➤ If you lose what you had and want to recover it, this is the time for a rebalance. Both the balance in a gait or in a movement can be difficult for the horse's mind and body to maintain, so recovery requires a rebalance. To successfully execute it requires practice and repetition.

➤ When you feel the horse going onto his forehand, this is the time to shift the weight back onto his hind legs by doing a rebalance.

➤ On the approach to a fence to maintain focus and quality of the gait. Often the gait deteriorates when the horse and rider's focus is transferred to the jump.

➤ On landing, the effort used in jumping becomes an interruption to what you had before the jump, so it has to be restored.

➤ Rebalances are useful when galloping because a balanced gallop is more economical than an unbalanced one. This, in turn, is better for the horse's efficiency in competition and for continued soundness.

The Rebalance: Questions for Riders to Ask Themselves

➤ What has prompted me to think there is a need to rebalance?

➤ What has happened to my horse's way of going that needs addressing?

➤ Is my coach encouraging me to rebalance or do I *feel* the need to do something?

Riding the Rebalance

The rebalance conversation has to make a connection in the horse's mind between your leg and his own hind end: leg–quarters–back–poll–jaw–bit–hand (fig. 9.3). This may range from a quiet "Hello" to a "Come here and let's talk."

As all rebalances happen when the horse's weight is moved from the front to the back, by "talking" to the hind legs, you warn them that they are needed to help take some of the weight. It is a mechanical process of redistribution. At the same time, the rein aids have a conversation with the horse's mouth, a conversation that says, "Do not misunderstand what the legs are asking; they are not saying go forward." As your legs ask, the rein aids must stop the horse's inclination to go. The result is that the hind legs do more work (underneath the horse) and start to take the weight off the front end, redistributing the weight to the place it was in before the loss of balance occurred.

9.3 **9.3 To have a horse feel "through," there needs to be a connection starting with your leg and ending at your hand.**

Some might say that a rebalance is a momentary happening, a mild "call to attention" for the horse, but it must be as positive and prolonged as it needs to be to get a reaction. Once a reaction has been offered, positive acknowledgment from you must be equally obvious.

When I ask riders how they half-halt I get many answers: "I massage the outside rein," "I lift my rib cage," "I use my hip bones," "I drive through my seat," "I bring my shoulders back and look upward for guidance." None of these make any connection to the hind legs, so for me they are all invalid. You can often be fooled into thinking the horse has rebalanced when he offers a slow-down, but you have to be careful of this because a horse slowing down still needs to redistribute his weight and become more actively involved from behind.

Often, riders resort to changing bits to "improve" this feel of slowing down. This becomes a false result—a result that can also be compounded as the horse braces against the bit but still only slows down. This is not what is wanted as the power from the horse's hind end does not become available to you. With three-ring bits or gags, for example, there is a delay to the response as the mouthpiece stretches the horse's lips to the point of reaction. The same "false economy" is true of double bridles. Just because riders have "control" doesn't mean that the right things happen. How often have you seen a horse with his head and neck in a fixed shape and nothing happening through his hind legs and back? Riders must feel that the horse isn't simply being blocked in front to produce a semblance of a rebalance, but that his whole body is part of the process and there is a genuine transfer of weight because both parties have understood what is needed.

The rebalance is a collection of aids applied almost together. The partnership must understand each one before the whole process can be understood.

Much is said and taught about the role of the seat in the rebalance, but so often neither horse nor rider—as individuals or a partnership—understand this concept. It has not become part of their vocabulary. Horses that don't understand "through" will respond to your seat by hollowing and losing the connection from the back to front. For this reason, the use of the seat in the rebalance should not be taught too early, but it can be very helpful as horse and rider become more educated.

> **The rebalance conversation has to make a connection in the horse's mind between your leg and his own hind end.**

If this sounds patronizing, I do not mean it that way. It is just that I hear so often that the seat does this and that, when in practice, it is doing the opposite. The same rider might ask me, "How do I get my horse off his forehand and engage his hind legs?"

This shows that the use of the rider's seat was doing nothing to help the rebalance that would bring the horse off the forehand. This misguided/misunderstood use of the seat can make these issues harder to solve.

It is the coach's responsibility to step in and guide the horse and rider through this blockage, which is often well intentioned, just mistimed. The layering of this next level of information has come too soon.

The same applies when talking about the subtle use of the outside rein in the rebalance. Teach it too soon and it becomes meaningless as it produces the same slowing-down reaction, but with no confirmation of the connection. Only when horse and rider truly understand the idea of "between *both* legs and *both* hands" can this next layer of information be contemplated. Used correctly, the outside rein can become a subtle refinement of the aid. Both legs and reins are still involved and the conversation has the same language, but there is a more subtle intonation and inference.

I hesitate to mention the "subtleties" as they are often immediately attempted as the first port of call. As soon as the educated horse understands to "keep coming" from the leg and that the rein aids mean "Whoa" not "Slow down," then it is often simply a thought that produces the desired result.

CHAPTER TEN

Dressage Outside the Arena

Where did we school before we had arenas? When I started out doing horses on my own I had no money to spend on luxuries such as arenas or lessons. My school became the road, some tracks nearby, and a grass triangle in the middle of a road junction.

I am well aware that with the increase in traffic and the roads becoming a less safe place to be this is not always possible, but riders should became creative in how they use their "facilities." When the road was quiet, I would leg-yield from one side to the other, use the hedge to help with my shoulder-in, the grass verge with a hill was good for medium trots, while the gullies in the grass became the young horses' first ditch.

When the ground was dry enough, I could use the field. None of my land was flat, so my canter circles improved the horse's balance. I used to watch Captain Ben Jones, Chief Instructor at the Royal Army Veterinary Corps Center, Melton Mowbray, working his mount Custer on the side of a hill in canter. He went uphill and downhill, all in perfect balance.

> **The horse should be dependent, in a good way, on where you guide him.**

No Arena? No Problem

Riders have become programmed to ride in a rectangle, along predestined lines, to markers that follow a pattern. They are taught to go from letter to letter in certain shapes. Horses as well as riders become programmed to this process of riding. They become familiar with where they are going and what is coming next. Sometimes, this is a good thing as much of their learning is done by the repetition of exercises. But other times, it is less than good because anticipation, although sometimes helpful, can also be a problem.

What if you didn't use a rectangle? Imagine riding in a field or in an irregular arena. What difference would it make to rider and horse? I believe it makes a huge difference to communication skills and to the horse's attention to those skills. Horses never become complacent because they never know where they are going or what they are doing until they are actually asked.

To start with there are no predefined lines other than the ones you have created. You actually have to think about where the boundaries are. There is not the luxury of running along the fence or white boards. The horse becomes dependent, in a good way, on where you guide him (fig. 10.1).

Riders must make their own markers—the yellow flower or the cow pat. These markers have to be explained to the horse by way of a pre-aid, before an action begins. Riders have to become more familiar with dimensions of shapes: What does a 10-, 15-, or 20-meter circle look like without the help of letters or fences? Is the shape symmetrical?

Why Surfaces Go Against Nature

The soundness benefits of working in fields are not to be underestimated. Horses have evolved over thousands of years and have limbs that are designed to function on natural and uneven ground. The feet and their associated joints, especially in the front limbs, are designed to absorb and disperse the pressures of movement. In doing so, the foot slides and spreads, the frog acts against the ground, and the horse slows down. At the same time, the ligaments that secure each joint are exercised, and in doing so, develop a tolerance to this movement.

When a horse works on a prepared surface, especially one that offers "spring and security," the absorption of movement is transferred to every joint up to the knees and hocks—exactly what was *not* designed to happen. The result can be an increased incidence of lameness.

Do not think a horse is too precious to go out; do not think it is kind to stay on a nice soft arena—it is not natural!

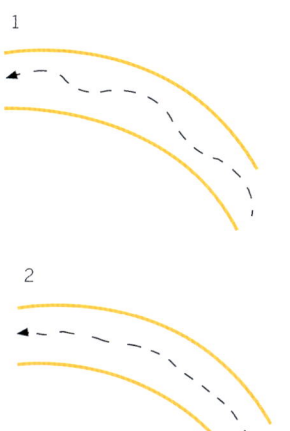

1

2

3

10.1 When working outside you must create your own boundaries and the horse must listen to where you guide him. The closer the boundaries, the straighter the horse becomes.

Riding becomes much more than just sitting on the horse. Every step has to be thought out. The horse is waiting for this input because in an open space he does not know, nor can he guess, as he did last time. So riding without boundaries becomes a much more involved process, one that improves the partnership and the interdependence between horse and rider. Try it for a few days and see what happens.

My own arena, by intent, isn't symmetrical. The variety of shapes I can ride is infinite. I do not have—and have never had—dressage letters, so I become more aware of markers in my mind. Straight lines are ridden by feel and by looking where I am going. Riding in a field is a joy and a challenge as it tests the joint understanding of what is going on.

If you follow this logic and encourage the horse to look along the line you are asking him to go, he continues the *buying-in* process. Make the line surprising, unlikely, or challenging, and the horse will trust you by going where you ask. This develops a bond that becomes more than just flatwork. The horse starts to look along the line to see what's coming. He takes an interest and gets ready to solve the puzzle. By opening his mind to being engaged, you have a horse thinking and looking ahead to when you add jumps into the equation. He becomes less surprised when this process continues on the cross-country course, which means you can ride tighter lines and take time-saving options.

Solving Flatwork Problems

Finding solutions to problems can be a fun challenge. Seldom do we buy, breed, or inherit a horse that doesn't have a small issue. Equally, riders can cause problems through misunderstanding.

Riders and coaches need to have a toolbox full of remedies. I have already mentioned the concept of a start point. When a problem arises, now is the time to see which start points are in place as you retrace your training steps to find out what is good in the training. Only then can you move forward again, having made the necessary corrections to put things right.

You must unravel the complications and get back to the simple things: forward, straight, and regular. Does the horse accept and understand the aids?

A Feel for the Great Outdoors

On two separate occasions, I had two of my Danish pupils visit for the summer. Neither was particularly used to riding outside an arena, but I like to get outside in the fields with my horses in the summer months. My Danish riders' horses were found wanting. They found it really difficult to balance and find their footing with the differing terrain. My riders were also lost as they now had to cope with horses that were finding it hard going. There was much uncertainty.

After about a week of acclimatization, the riders began to look and think ahead, make plans, help their horses up and down slopes, canter circles on slopes, and generally start "feeling" more.

I was able to watch the horses draw their hind legs underneath them to improve their balance and start listening more to their riders because they needed to know which direction to go. It was a win-win situation.

Q I struggle with riding downward transitions into walk because my horse either jogs or stops too abruptly. What can I do to improve this?

A Before beginning the correction process, you need to ask yourself: how does a good transition look? The horse should have an attentive expression on his face and he should look forward with an interest in going somewhere. When a light leg aid is applied, he should briskly walk forward with purpose. Ideally, he should be on the bit. The faults you mention are common. The horse shows resistance to the contact, goes hollow through his back, and stops going forward with swing into the walk.

Most faults are caused by the training, so it is important to really engage the horse's brain when trying to correct things. Try to put him in a situation that encourages him to retrain himself. A small circle in trot will make him want to walk, so he will offer a transition. At the same time he will rebalance himself, which will allow you to apply a leg aid asking him to go forward into the transition. A still, quiet, and mildly resistant rein aid will assist him doing what he wants to do anyway. If you are working by yourself, you must identify when the horse has given you the correct response and reward him. When it doesn't work, try to identify which part of it faltered and what you need to do about it. Prioritize the faults and be prepared to solve one at a time before piecing the whole jigsaw puzzle together.

> It is important to really engage the horse's brain when trying to correct faults.

Q My horse is slow to react to my leg when I ask him for a walk-trot transition. He also comes against the hand and falls left. How can I resolve this?

A You need to aim for a walk that remains purposeful with no change to the frame when the horse takes a crisp step forward into trot. Begin a conversation with the leg aids and be ready to react to the horse's response. If he is slow to the leg, deal with it using the spur, stick, or voice, and then return to walk. Carry on walking and then ask again with a light aid. If nothing changes, deal with it by having a little "louder" conversation. When the horse responds to a light aid, reward him. Then repeat the process.

Maintain a quiet contact, but don't allow him to go against the hand into trot—he is only allowed to trot when he is quick from the leg and accepting of the hand. The falling left is not the priority and will correct itself as the other faults are removed.

Q When I try to go into canter my horse trots faster and faster. How do I stop him doing this?

A To achieve a clear, crisp transition into canter the horse needs to accept and understand the conversation the leg and hand are having. When I work on trot-canter transitions, I have a list of priorities. These are:

The outline: This is non-negotiable and must stay the same; a slight speeding up is acceptable if the outline remains accepting. The transition should not be accepted at the expense of the horse going above the bit.

Resistance to the leg: This needs to be discussed and negotiated by the legs (in the same way as the walk-trot transition). Crisp and clean often happens later when the other issues are dealt with.

Falling right or left: This is easy to resolve later. Prioritize the first two points, so you allow the horse to order his own thoughts. He, too, can then prioritize the order in which he finds the correct solution. This mind mapping is as important to him as it is to us.

Q Judges always remark on my test sheet that my horse "falls into trot" and is "on his forehand." What does this mean and how can I rectify it?

A A good downward transition should begin with an obvious rebalance that allows the horse to control the momentum and begin the new gait correctly. The horse needs to allow himself to be "talked to" before he is asked the real question. This conversation is a warning that something is about to happen and there is a need to get ready. Without this conversation, or when the horse doesn't listen, things fall apart.

To begin the conversation, apply the leg aids closely followed by a resistant rein aid, saying to the horse, "Hind legs under, lighten the front."

As the horse acknowledges this, it will allow you to *ride* the transition as opposed to sitting on top, hoping it will happen. Remember, a transition is not the end of one gait, it is the beginning of the next. Proactive riding will always help.

Q **My coach often remarks that I sit to the right, but I can't seem to shift my weight over and stay there. Is it really that important?**

 The rider should sit centrally to ensure an even distribution of weight and give the horse the best chance of being in balance. Sitting to the right or left is a common fault (fig. 10.2 A), as is being behind or in front of the movement. Solving the problem is almost a book in itself, but as a coach I look at it in a realistic way and ask, "What is it possible to improve on?" One of the start points for finding a more central balance is the platform—the stirrup. How the foot rests in it is critical. Too deep a heel creates imbalance, too high a heel creates a different imbalance. Solve the issue from the stirrup upward.

> A transition is not the end of one gait, it is the beginning of the next.

That said, I do not try to change things if biomechanics are against the rider. I also try not to create a rider fixation at the expense of communication and enjoyment. I try to prioritize and feed in long-term objectives. If, in doing this, riders feel they want to take on the task of change, then I can help them. If they do not want to change, it is important to work with what we have. Many older riders feel unwilling to undertake this change.

10.2 A & B
This rider is sitting to one side, which has caused the horse to lose straightness (A). When she corrects her position, the horse automatically becomes straight (B).

Q I need to work on my horse's straightness, especially on the center-line. What do I need to be thinking about?

A Being straight means the horse's hindquarters follow the forehand and follow the head on any line you choose (fig. 10.2 B). Common faults include the horse's hindquarters being to the inside of the line, too much bend, and the horse falling out through the outside shoulder.

To solve the problem you need to work on being able to move each of the three main parts of the horse independently, the three parts being: the hindquarters up to the saddle, the forehand including the rider, and the neck and head. Having achieved this, you must then define the line on which you wish to travel and keep the horse's spine on that line. There is no reason to have more bend to the inside than the line requires, while the outside aids should control the amount of bend and the horse's outside shoulder. On the centerline there is no need for bend; a very slight inclination of the direction to come will be enough.

When the hindquarters come in, avoid the temptation to push them back out. It is better to bring the forehand in front of the hindquarters and then move the whole horse back on the chosen line. This is easier said than done, though, so don't under-estimate the task. In the long term, however, you will be rewarded with a straighter horse (fig. 10.3).

As a footnote to the above, I do wish dressage judges would stop writing "More bend required" on dressage sheets. So many riders come home confused and set about asking their horses for more and more bend, when really they should be asking for better straightness.

10.3 A pleasing picture of horse and rider in harmony. Note the horse's expression of attention; the rider's still and quiet hand to the still and quiet mouth of the horse.

Pole Work

The world-famous Cadre Noir of Saumur, France, always has jumps and poles in the dressage training area. When horses become a little jaded, or need to be refreshed, or even just taught another way, the jumps and poles are always available.

I too always have poles dotted around my arena. They have many uses, add interest to flatwork, and can open doors into the Horse House (see p. 34).

Exercises in Walk

Scattered poles improve the horse's spatial awareness, decision-making skills, and independence.

When a horse walks over a pole on the ground he normally looks down at it and stretches his neck. This is a good reaction and should be encouraged. In this shape, when the horse lifts his front legs, he is loose and free of resistance in his shoulders. As you whisper to him with leg aids that say, "Keep doing what you are doing," the horse lifts his hind legs and possibly his back, without resistance. Now the pole has produced a horse in the correct shape and listening to your quiet aid. This is a super beginning to *all* work and a precursor to good jumping later on when more information can be layered on.

Try the following:

➤ Once the horse is quietly walking over a pole, start to aim for a specific point on the pole—a color, a mark, or something else that is measurable. Now we have increased the information we have given to the horse—the need to ride to a line or marker.

➤ Add in a turn before the pole. The leg aids are now being used more independently with an offering rein added for direction. More accuracy is needed from you, while the horse is required to be more aware of his inside hind leg.

➤ Add a change of direction. As the horse crosses the pole, you should change your leg aids to ask for a change of rein. You must coordinate your aids, while the horse must understand and coordinate his body to comply with the request. Now the horse's other hind leg becomes more active as it becomes the new inside leg.

Other ways to use walk poles:

Walk Grid Poles

Create a walk grid by scattering poles close together, but still with no set distance between them and no shape to their layout. Walk the horse through the grid and ask yourself to feel how you look, plan, and find your way through (fig. 11.1 A). This can also be done in trot (fig. 11.1 B). This simple

11.1 A & B By placing poles randomly on the ground, the horse has to focus on his footwork (A). The same exercise can be done in trot, but now the horse must make decisions more quickly (B).

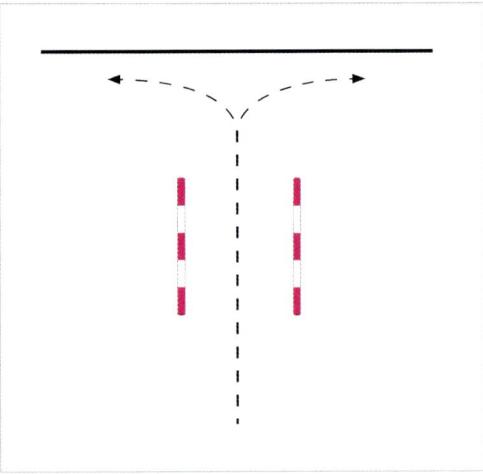

11.2 Using boundary poles helps focus your mind and improve the horse's attentiveness.

exercise is really helpful for improving the horse's spatial awareness, decision-making skills, and independence.

Parallel Poles

I tend to use flat poles or laths for this exercise to avoid the horse standing on something round.

Set up two parallel poles about 3 feet (1m) apart and walk between them (fig. 11.2). Then narrow the gap to 2 feet 6 inches (80cm). The horse should begin to look at the line ahead of him and *buy in* to what is being asked. He is listening to the aids, which are asking him to stay between the poles. His understanding is continually improving and he is developing trust in what you are asking.

Boundary Poles

Use two parallel poles facing the fence, which acts as a boundary—somewhere for you to aim at (see fig. 11.2). You will need to coordinate your aids to make sure you get a response between the poles. The horse sees why he has to listen because he knows that something will happen at this point.

This exercise helps the horse's speed of reaction, his understanding of the aids, and his interest. He is *buying in*. It also helps you speed up your coordination and understanding of your aids.

Halting Over a Pole

Asking for halt over a pole has many benefits. The timing and coordination of your aid are tested. So, too, is the horse's understanding of the aid that is being applied and his belief that you really mean it.

As the horse walks over the pole, you should only ask for halt one in every three or so times. This means the horse will keep thinking forward and continue to bring the hind legs under himself. As you think halt and apply the aid, the horse is still thinking walk, so the hind legs are more likely to come in square. Another good link in the horse's mind has been made—your legs influencing the horse's hind legs.

Exercises in Trot

When introducing a young horse to poles he should be allowed to stretch down his neck and look. He has to assess the poles and work out where to place his feet. By lowering his neck he is using the muscles of his topline, which has many benefits in the way he carries himself and you. It also develops the correct way of going. You need to ensure that the contact is never lost, but as the horse looks and stretches, you must allow with the hands and follow the contact with the horse's mouth.

The horse needs to be allowed to assess the poles and work out where to place his feet.

11.3 This horse is listening to his rider and showing a good frame for working over trot poles.

As the horse becomes more understanding of poles and developed in his way of going, it is beneficial to change this long, low frame and ask for a normal working-trot frame (fig. 11.3). For a horse to hold himself and know where his feet are being placed is challenging, but it works a different balance in the partnership and introduces the concept of more collection. Poles can be used on a straight line or a curve. Both are beneficial. Like in walk, aiming for a specific place on the pole will focus you on maintaining a chosen line.

Knowing when, why, and how to use trotting poles is the key to gaining

11.4 Using poles on a circle helps improve balance, elasticity of the step, and self-carriage.

the greatest benefit. The simple and obvious reason for using them is to regulate the trot. So much can be layered on top of this.

Use Trot Poles...to Aid Lengthening and Shortening

Changing the distance between the poles means making the horse's stride longer or shorter. This is a good exercise for many reasons, including improving the elasticity of the step, the ability to stretch, and promoting better self-carriage (fig. 11.4).

As you become more creative and thoughtful in their use, it is possible to introduce other ideas that can improve impulsion, cadence, balance, contact, connection, physical development of the topline, and the approach/takeoff and getaway from a jump.

Use Trot Poles...to Improve Physical Agility and Core Strength

Raising alternate ends of a row of trotting poles tests the mental and physical agility of the horse, who has to be aware of which pole is raised, react accordingly, and be quick with his footwork. This further improves the neurological pathways of the aids (fig. 11.5).

A normal trot stride for an average-sized horse (16 hands) is between 4–5 feet (1.2–1.5m). When used in a circle, like spokes of a wheel, the poles should be closer together toward the inside, but never wider than 5 feet (1.5m) on the outside.

Use more than two poles for this exercise; otherwise the horse is likely to jump them.

The next layer of the exercise is to raise the poles at both ends. It is important not to get too ambitious and think that the higher the pole the greater the benefit—this is not so. A height of 9–10 inches (23–25cm) is enough.

The distance between the poles will vary according to the size of horse and the desired result.

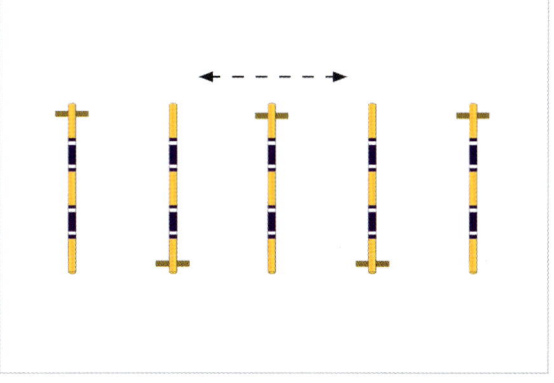

11.5 Poles raised on 4- to 6-inch (10–15cm) blocks (that do not allow the poles to move) on one side, like these, can help the horse improve his footwork. This further develops correct neurological pathways of the aids.

Raised poles exercise the horse's joints and develop his core strength. He must remain forward in his mind, straight, and regular. He should also be secure between the aids.

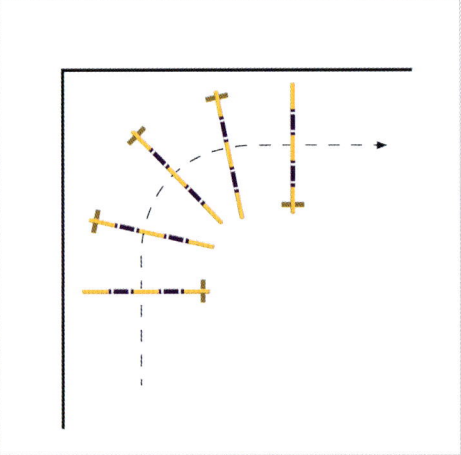

11.6 Placing poles, either flat or raised on one side, around a corner encourages the horse to remain forward and regular.

Use Trot Poles...to Improve Corners

When riding into the corner of a dressage arena, the line is a small quarter-of-a-circle. Most horses and riders find this a challenge to do well—losing balance and impulsion are the main issues. Poles can help with this.

Place three poles in the corner (distances as above), but not so near to the boundary that it is beyond the angle of corner the horse would be expected to go.

Trotting through the poles while riding the corner will encourage improved balance and self-carriage because the horse has to trust that he can still remain forward and regular as he negotiates the exercise.

As the horse gets used to this, add an extra two poles (fig. 11.6).

The next stage is to raise the inside of poles 1 and 5 and the outside of poles 2, 3 and 4. This will have the effect of guiding the horse into the exercise and hence the corner.

Use Trot Poles...to Help Transitions

Much can be achieved by asking for a transition in front of a pole. Start with trot-walk-trot transitions before moving on into canter-trot transitions (figs. 11.7 A & B).

Begin by asking for a transition close enough to the pole that it is still related, but far enough away that its quality can be retained. As the transition improves, it can be moved closer to the poles—12–15 feet (4–5m) away, for example. The horse will focus on the impending poles, but at the same time he will have to think about the transition—he is having to multitask.

The above will allow you to feed in a rebalance at the very time it might need to appear in front of a jump later on.

Transitions can also be done after the poles, which will help encourage the horse to be attentive to your aids while looking after his main job—the poles. This will be helpful when rebalancing after a jump.

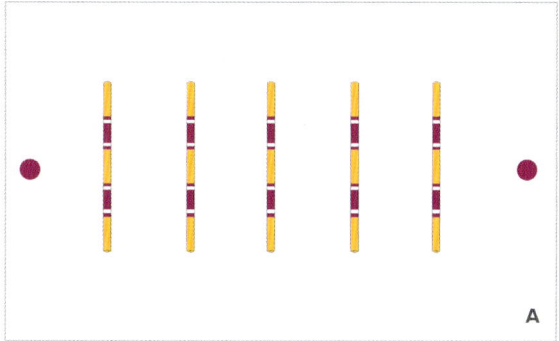

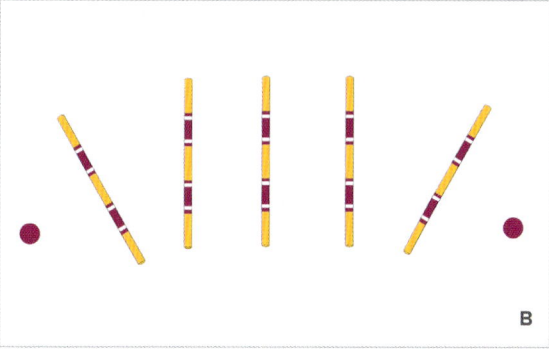

11.7 A & B Asking for transitions before and after a line of poles (indicated by dots) requires the horse to be attentive to the rider's aids (A). By pulling out the first and last poles a little, the horse's balance is challenged (B).

CHAPTER TWELVE

Jumping in the Arena

Much is written about the art of jumping—mostly by people who are good at it. The difficulty is that a lot of talented jumping riders cannot fathom how others can't do as they can.

I was once told by a top show jumper with whom I had a lesson, "Look, Eric, you've got to see a better spot, about a foot closer to the fence!" I couldn't see any spot let alone a better one and certainly not one a foot closer! (A "spot" or "stride" or "distance" is the best place for the horse to take off.) I was already competing at a high level at this stage and was embarrassed to admit my failures.

Before I took up horses professionally, I had been told what "great feel" I had to a jump. But once I started being trained my confidence disappeared because of how I was taught. I felt I had to see something that I found difficult to see. I had to ride strides and distances that I found hard. I kept trying to find a better way.

So much of what is taught about jumping is about how to arrive at the fence, but this creates too much emphasis on seeing a stride. Most people can't "see" and it is not fair to tell them they have to learn!

If I want a rider to improve, I redirect her focus; find a different way. I am asked more times than I can recount to teach people to see a stride. Yet without me once saying "stride" for the next hour, they go away happy, jumping fence after fence without a care in the world. This is because I redirect their focus.

I spend enough time standing beside fences listening to riders' huffs and puffs of discontent to know when riders are not happy. Even when a jump stays

> **Most people can't "see" a distance to a fence, and it is not fair to tell them they have to learn!**

up some appear less than pleased. Seeking perfection is always elusive and it becomes even more so when riders believe they have done a less than perfect job. This lack of confidence and belief surely stems from the system in which they are trained. It certainly compounds the problem. The way some coaches teach does nothing to make it easier for horses and riders to arrive at the fence in the best way to jump it. I say this because when I teach new pupils, hear the murmurs of discontent, and ask the question, "Have you been taught to look for a stride?" they almost always answer, "Yes, but I have great difficulty seeing one."

It is important to address the psychology of jumping. When riders cannot see a stride, but feel they are in the minority, they begin to develop a complex about not *seeing*. If they do not admit to being unable to see, then the complex becomes more deeply ingrained. It was only when I admitted to myself that I needed to change something that I became more comfortable about not *seeing* any more than about 70 percent of the jumps I approached. When I appreciated that there was another way to jump without seeing all the jumps perfectly, I stopped looking and started riding. Then nearly all my anxieties disappeared.

The Five Phases of Jumping

To understand how to achieve a better result without worrying about seeing strides, it is helpful to break down jumping into five distinct phases: the approach, the takeoff, in the air, the landing, and the getaway (figs. 12.1–12.5).

You need to keep uppermost in your mind that all jumping revolves around two qualities: *line* and *pace*. At this stage I should say that for the rest of the book all jumps will be jumped from the canter gait. The word "pace" will describe the speed and quality of the canter gait. Let's look more closely.

1 The Approach
The first phase is very important and has various components (see fig. 12.1):

The line: In the early learning stages course designers will set lines that are straightforward, normally giving riders enough time between the jumps to recover the quality of the canter before the next fence. As the horse and rider's education improves, so the jumps come up more quickly and the lines become more difficult to ride, challenging the rider's ability before they even present to a fence.

It is in everybody's interests to try and simplify each line. Like in dressage, there are lines that should be followed, but unlike in dressage, there is more choice when negotiating a course of fences: lines that are possible to do, lines the horse jumps better from, and lines that save time. Every line chosen must have logic and a plan—not just because that's what expected, but because it suits horse and rider.

The gait and pace: For most jumps the gait is the canter. Regardless of the chosen line, the canter must be the very best quality possible to give the horse the best chance of jumping the jump. The gait should be uninterrupted, so sharp corners and obvious rebalances need to be avoided. Counting the last three strides is also unproductive, as it often leads to three-two-one-oh...shoot! If you know you are going to be right when you start counting then there is no point in counting! If you don't know where you are, then counting doesn't help!

> **Visually and mentally, the horse must feel— and where possible see—that there is a plan and that he has a part in it.**

Don't count.

The horse must be allowed to focus solely on the job in hand—that of jumping. By giving him a sense of going somewhere, it improves his *buying in* to the process. Visually and mentally, the horse must feel—and where possible see—that there is a plan and that he has a part in it.

2 The Takeoff

This is always a source of much angst, but it need not be if the approach has been good (see fig. 12.2). A lot happens at this time and the partnership needs to know who does what.

➤ When does responsibility pass from rider to horse?

➤ Who does what?

12.1 The approach: Your job is to control the line and pace of the gait.

12.2 The takeoff: In the last few strides before takeoff, the horse should take an interest as you pass over responsibility for the jump.

12.3 In the air: You should focus on staying in balance and allowing the horse to do his job.

12.4 The landing: The rider starts to take back control.

12.5 The getaway: The sooner the canter is reestablished, the better the approach to the next fence will be.

> ➤ What is supposed to happen?

> ➤ Direction on landing?

> ➤ What happens if...?

You are in charge at all times, but must feel the horse taking an interest and ultimately taking over in the last few strides before a jump. It is important to ensure the horse does this as it is his job. Some horses are better at making this decision than others. You can help in the decision-making process, but must not make the decision for the horse. It is a fine line.

As the takeoff happens, you can quietly convey the direction on landing. This should not be done too aggressively or it will interrupt the jump—just enough to give the horse an indication.

The "What if" scenario happens when the horse does not make a decision. You must try and feel it before it happens to avoid a stop or a knock-down. The horse needs reminding that it is his job to make a plan and jump cleanly. This can be done with a kick, a tap with the stick, or a growl. It needs to be something to quickly gain the horse's attention. When the exercise is repeated, you should expect the horse to make an effort to jump. It needs to be made clear that on takeoff, he is expected to make and execute a plan.

There are many benefits to this joint responsibility. The rider knows that a good canter will put you in a reasonable area and that the horse will then take over to make the fine adjustments to jump the fence. You must not get in front of the horse's thought process of taking-off, nor get left behind. This is a moment to be practiced over small jumps to develop this feel. Once achieved, the reward is a feeling of being in a true partnership.

3 In the Air

This is the time for you to avoid distracting the horse, stay in balance, and interfere as little as possible (see fig. 12.3). The horse is trying to jump the fence clear and does not need you throwing your weight around. To stay in balance requires a position with a solid foundation. Any necessary movement from the rider should be in keeping with what the horse has to do to jump the fence. Negotiating a 3-foot (1m) fence is different from leaping over 5 feet (1m 60).

In the air is also a time that the direction of travel can be confirmed to the horse, having already hinted to him on takeoff. You need to look where you want to go, offer the lead rein, and put pressure on the stirrup, "stepping into" the new direction.

4 The Landing

This phase is more important than many riders imagine (see fig. 12.4). You have to reestablish responsibility for the next phase—the getaway—and remain in balance. Staying off the horse's back and being subtle with the aids as you take back responsibility can be a challenge. The horse has to follow through and ensure his hind legs have cleared the fence, so you must not upset this process.

> The landing phase of the jump is more important than many riders imagine.

The first stride after the landing needs to be positive to ensure it is not short and lacking in energy. Too much "drive" spoils this stride; too little, and the quality of the getaway is diminished.

Poles can be useful to help with this. Place a pole between 12–14 feet (3.7–4.3m) from the base of the landing side of the jump—be careful not to put it any closer as it may encourage the horse to jump it—and a second pole a further 12 feet away. This will improve the quality of the first two strides of the getaway.

5 The Getaway

Stride one after the fence should always be good because this provides a solid beginning for the rest of the getaway (see fig. 12. 5). Total "order" to the canter may take two or three strides to achieve, but the sooner you have reestablished the canter the better, as this becomes the approach to the next jump.

As these five phases demonstrate, there is a continuing transfer of responsibility between the two partners—horse and rider. For this to happen smoothly, practice is necessary and clarity of these roles needs to be established. Any lack of clarity leads to confusion, which, in turn, leads to poor jumping and a loss of trust.

Geometry and Jumping

I am conscious that in most training systems riders have been taught to ride in a straight line toward a fence, and that each straight line should be preceded by a corner, where the horse is balanced and "set up" in preparation for leaving the ground. The rider is encouraged to "see a stride" and make any necessary adjustments so that the arrival at the fence is "correct." This seems to be a pre-programmed process.

Increasingly, though, I have found this does not work. In fact, I believe it has so many flaws that it inhibits people from jumping to their full potential. Here is why:

1 Riding a corner can improve the horse's balance, but it can also cause a loss of balance, interrupt the quality of the canter, and kill the impulsion. The aim is to arrive at the point of takeoff with the very best canter possible and so give the horse the greatest chance of jumping cleanly. Having broken the flow at this critical moment by riding a corner, what might have been a really good canter is now lost; the result is that the rider either "holds" or "chases" in an effort to try to recover the canter. Neither works.

2 To set up for a fence is yet another interruption to the canter, which may have been good in the first place. For the rider to set up because she believes she should is yet another interruption to the partnership's focus.

3 Seeing a spot or looking for a distance causes more anxiety than just about any other subject in riding. I have already mentioned this, and in all my coaching I try to wean riders and coaches off the concept.

The Alternative Way

Racecar drivers are able to maintain power through a bend so as not to surrender precious seconds by drifting, spinning, or losing balance. They do this by choosing a gear and a speed that is appropriate for the track they are driving. Riders need to do something similar.

Rather than trying to ride corners and tight turns, I believe riders should be focusing on executing continuous lines with no interruption to the balance, in a canter that is being continually assessed and improved or maintained. At the same time the horse should be encouraged to *buy in* to seeing where he is in front of the fence and following the line. This becomes a win-win situation because riders can build on what they *can* do rather than struggling with something they find difficult. I like to think of the idea as the "Deadman's Corner" versus the "Wiseman's Curve" (figs. 12.6 A & B).

> **When jumping, there is a continuing transfer of responsibility between horse and rider.**

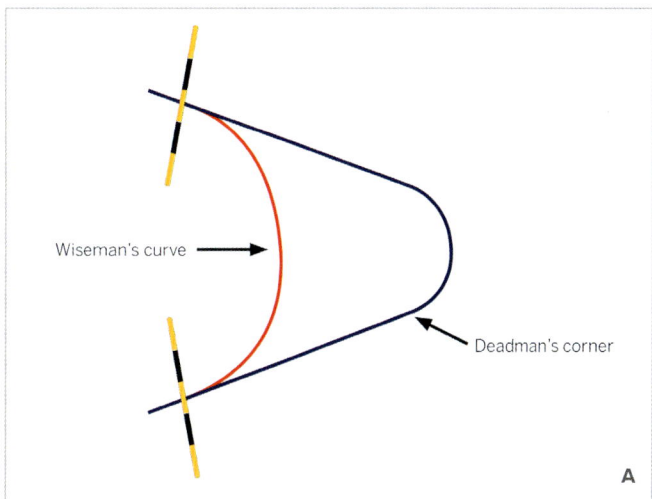

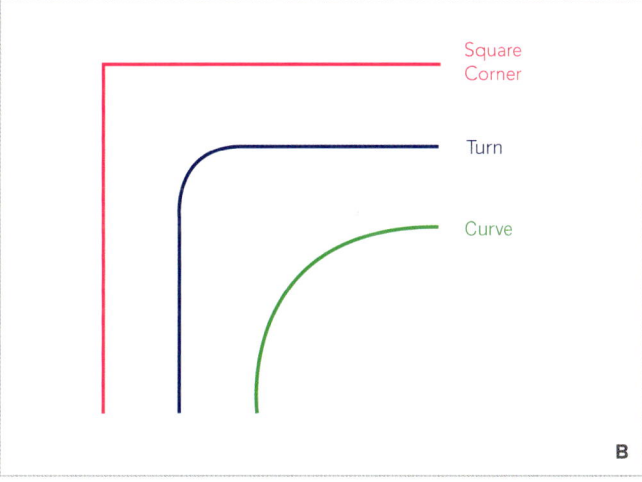

12.6 A & B Following the red line (Wiseman's curve) allows for a smoother approach than trying to ride the blue line (Deadman's corner) (A). Talking terminology: riding a square corner approach (the most difficult), a turn (tricky), and a curve (the easiest) (B).

So, where do you start?

In dressage, a lot of time is spent perfecting the canter and riding circles. There should be the same focus when jumping. On the flat, all sorts of sized circles can be ridden, but for jumping between 12 and 20 meters is best. Start by aiming to increase and decrease the size of the circle without losing the quality of the canter. By retaining forwardness, straightness, and regularity you now have a pace and a line that will allow horse and rider to cope with the vast majority of jumps—without having to see anything!

Using Circle Lines to Help the Approach

The Canter Circle

1 Place a single pole at a point around a 20-meter circle. Get used to cantering over one pole at a time before adding a second at the opposite point on the circle.

2 Ensure that you ride the canter not the pole. Don't be concerned about "getting it right" at the pole, your task is simply to make sure the quality of the canter and the shape of the circle remains.

> **Rather than trying to ride corners and tight turns, riders should focus on executing continuous lines with no interruption to the balance.**

3 Two more poles can now be added at the four circle points. It will be tempting for you to adjust the canter to make it "right" for the horse if he starts kicking or standing on the poles, but this is counterproductive. The aim is to encourage the horse to make a decision about where he puts his feet.

4 The two opposite poles can now be raised into small jumps (fig. 12.7). As the regularity of the canter is maintained so the ability to "feel" the canter improves, and the relationship between jumps starts to develop. Guide poles can be helpful to clarify the line (fig. 12.8).

5 Most horses will put four or five strides between the poles/fences on a 20-meter circle, but the number of strides is not important so long as

the canter is regular and remains of a good quality. The horse will begin to *buy in* to the exercise and look along the curved line for the jump.

6 This exercise also teaches the horse to think about his balance and what to do with his feet and canter lead on landing. The expression, "Follow the lead rein" is now easy to understand.

7 Rider position is important. I advocate a light seat—not forward, nor sitting. You need to be able to respond quickly and quietly, staying in balance on takeoff, but at the same time staying very slightly behind the horse to ensure the horse stays forward. Now you and the horse have every chance of the best possible approach.

The Sombrero

1 As the jumps become higher, it is easier for the horse to have one or two straight strides in front of the jump. Enter the sombrero! This is when I draw a sombrero shape in the arena surface or put a marker at a spot one or two horse strides, 12–24 feet (3.7–

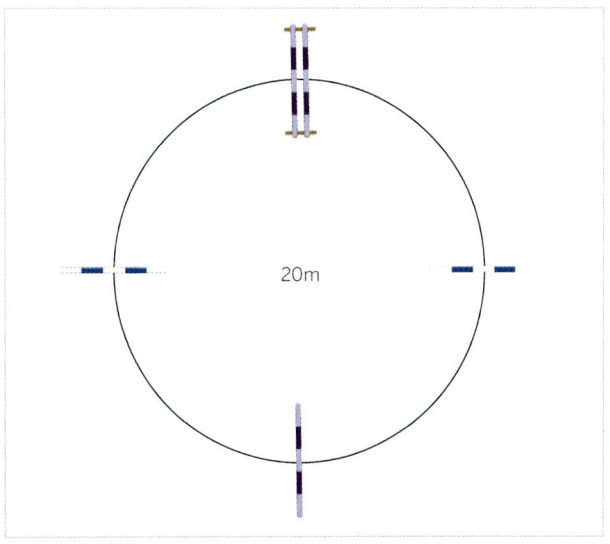

12.7 One of my favorite exercises is building up from one pole to four fences on a circle.

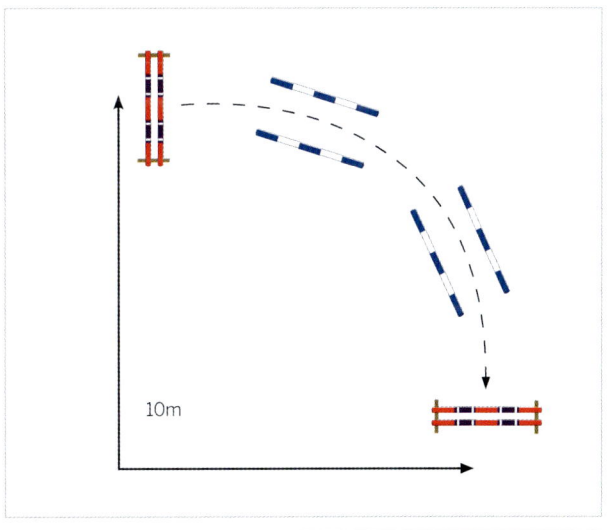

12.8 Guide poles can be used to help guide the horse around the circle.

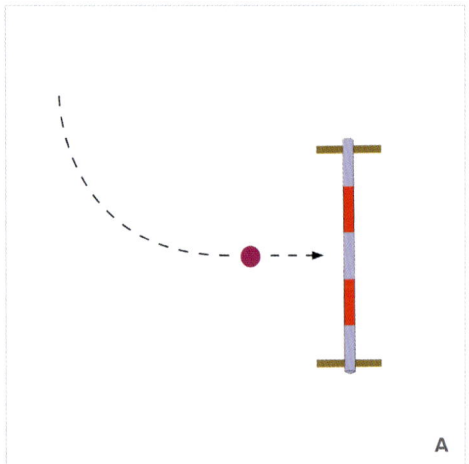

12.9 A & B Marking a point in front of the fence (I call this a "sombrero") improves your focus and the canter (A). The sombrero seen in the sand. Also see the raked path through the poles in the foreground (B).

7.3m), from the fence, which becomes a visual reference point for you to ride to (figs. 12.9 A & B).

2 The same curved approach should be ridden, but now the target is the sombrero rather than the jump. This visualization is very important and it should become one of the strongest thoughts in your mind. Actively "riding" the line and knowing where it is taking the horse improves the focus and the canter.

3 The positioning of the sombrero as a reference point can be changed to suit different horses' needs and minds.

4 Eventually, it will become a "mental" sombrero rather than a physical marker.

5 The quicker the horse becomes at making takeoff decisions, the closer to the one-stride marker the mental sombrero becomes. It may take a young horse or slower-brained horse a little longer to make the correct takeoff decision, so you should move the mental focus back accordingly.

The Benefits of Curves

A little while ago I received this email from one of my pupils, Danish rider and trainer Tine Lyders Larsen. I thought it was worth sharing:

"My pupils had cut a perfect square in a field with a lawn mower and built a jumping course with a lot of perfect straight lines. It was beautiful. It fit perfectly into my mathematical mind, and at the same time, it provoked me. So I changed everything to curved lines. The result was amazing. I usually think that I do not have enough fences, yet it seemed that I had a thousand lines to work with.

"I have often found it difficult to persuade riders to leave the responsibility of jumping to the horse, but by riding curved lines it became far easier. Horses really do rebalance themselves in a very different way.

"I was still impressed to see this change happening not only with one horse, but with a string of them. I have been wondering if I was capable of applying your theory to my teaching, and today it was easy."

Figures 12.11 A & B are two simple jump layouts to practice jumping off curves and circle lines. Figure 12.11 C shows another setup with numerous line options. How many can you see?

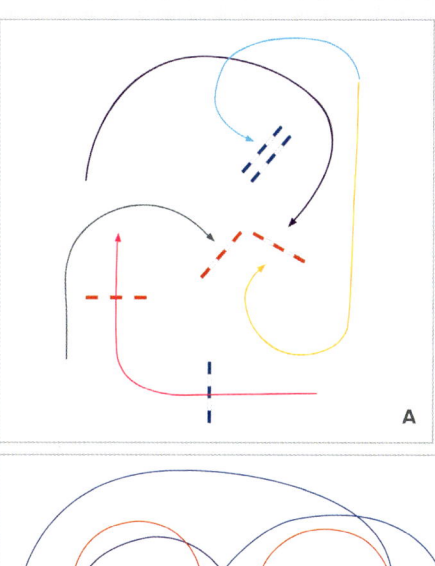

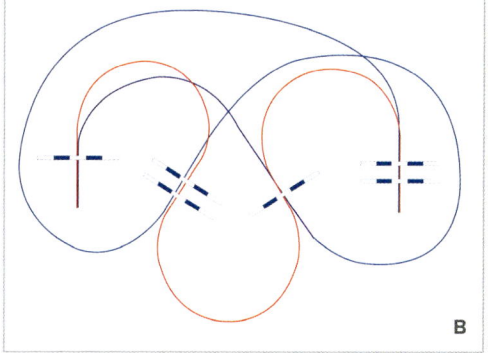

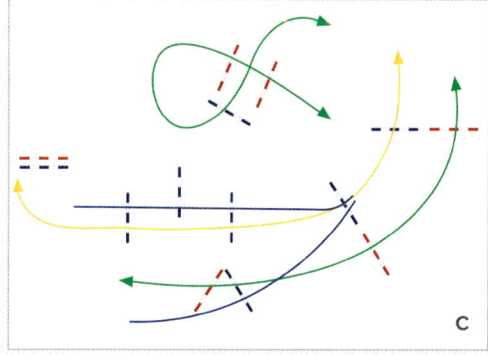

12.11 A–C This simple configuration gives the rider numerous opportunities to practice riding curves and half-circles (A). A setup can contain both easier and trickier curves and half-circles. The colored lines indicate different tracks you can follow (B). An interesting setup with some example lines you can ride. How many different options can you see (C)?

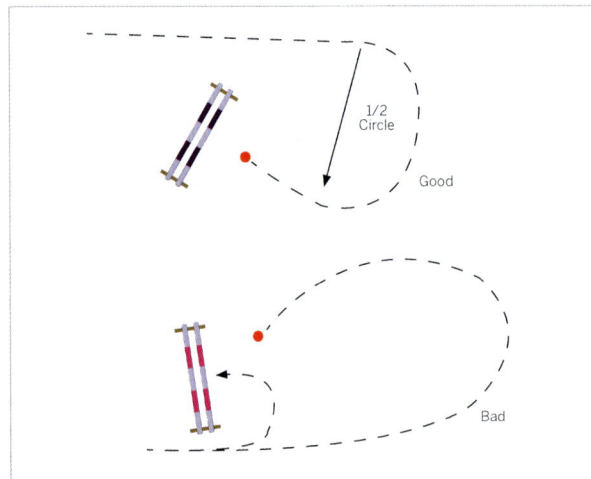

12.10 Riding half-circle lines to successfully tackle rollback fences.

The Roll Back

This is where you must make almost a complete turn back from one fence to the next and it is a line that course designers use to test balance, use of space, judgment of pace, and the ability to ride a line. The circle or half-circle will be the basis for this type of question, so it is important that you practice these shapes (fig. 12.10).

Throughout these exercises it is important for you to ask, "Is this canter good enough?" This will prompt a second question, "Good enough for what?" Good enough for the next jump. If at any stage it is *not* good enough, it must be improved. When it is good enough, you need to be busy keeping it that way until the next fence.

Many people say things to themselves in an effort to keep the quality of the canter as they go between jumps. This can be a useful tool provided that what is said is not confusing. It is not a good idea to count numbers because this can very easily be related in the subconscious to counting strides, which will not be helpful.

Look...Jump

There are so many different ways to reach the same goal of encouraging horses to look, assess, and jump, all of which are part of jumping cleanly, jumping safely, and having fun. I find this one of the most interesting stages in a horse's education. There are certain factors that remain critical in reaching this goal:

1 The horse has to say "I can."

2 He must have a desire to find a solution to the question.

3 He must make decisions on his own.

You want the horse to take a fence on, but it must be done in a way that combines keenness to go and do, while at the same time having a care and understanding of what is being asked. It is an interesting quality to train and I always have in mind the two extremes of the process: the horse that doesn't go and the horse that goes too much.

With the one that doesn't go, I ask, why not? Most horses like to jump, so you need to ensure this willingness is present at the beginning.

When working with poles or jumping, I begin with a single pole before progressing to a small cross-rail or single rail. The word and quality "forward" should always be in your mind. The horse must retain the feeling of taking you to the jump. Even if he looks when he gets there, he must keep going.

As this becomes clear to the horse he may misinterpret the concept by going too quickly. I always have a couple of jumps in the arena that I call "brake jumps"—jumps that are spooky, different, or in an awkward place. These allow me to put the horse in a situation where he slows himself down and does not rely on me to regulate the speed. In doing this, I am reminding him that even though I am asking him to take the fence on, he must also be patient, look, and assess.

> **The horse must understand that, when jumping, he must be patient, look, and assess.**

Approaching at the correct speed will give the horse time to make choices: too slow and he will not have enough impulsion; too fast and he has fewer choices and will end up too long, too close, or too flat. None of these makes jumping easy. A change to the speed means the horse must change his plans at the last minute, which again is not helpful.

Riders must have confidence not to change this speed either intentionally or unintentionally as this uncertainty is difficult for the horse to deal with. It also increases the uncertainty for the next jump—now the horse doesn't know what to expect and so the uncertainty is compounded.

Mental Gymnastics

Understanding gymnastic jumping is important as it plays a part in the mental and physical development of the horse. If you ask the horse a question, you must be sure that his mind can solve it. There must be certain functions already in place; otherwise he won't know how. It is fair to ask a little more than where these functions have already taken the horse, so long as you follow a logical line of questioning. When used well and with thought, gymnastic exercises can enhance good training and reinforce good neurological pathways. When used badly, they can close a horse's mind to finding a solution and so risk his "I can" attitude.

Gymnastic exercises can also be used by the lazy coach to produce a "wow factor" by jumping a big fence at the end of the line. This often excites everyone, but gives the rider a false feeling of competence as she is still no better at cantering to a single vertical of 3 feet (90cm). Meanwhile, the horse had nothing more to decide other than to take off.

There is undoubtedly a place for gymnastics, but they are not everything we wish for. There may be a time and a place in the horse's education when they are appropriate, but they should be used with caution.

> **There may be a time and a place in the horse's education when gymnastics are appropriate, but they should be used with caution.**

There are so many different gymnastic exercises that it is beyond the scope of this book to cover them all. Every trainer will have his favorite exercises and promote these, but their function is more important than the setup.

Gymnastic exercises are designed to encourage the horse to solve a problem and answer a question. He has to use his brain and move his feet in order to get through the exercise. By doing it right, he will develop correct neurological pathways, which, if repeated regularly, become a good habit and one that is able to be used instinctively, without much—if any—cognitive thought.

To do gymnastics badly often produces a mental attitude that says, "I see a problem that is too difficult to solve!" Now, when presented with a question, the closed mind says, "I can't," before it says, "Maybe," or "I can." This uncertainty translates into a stop or hesitation at the jump, or worse still, a half effort resulting in hitting an obstacle. If it is a solid fence the repercussions can be serious. When a horse is not able, unwilling, or just too confused to solve the question that you are asking, it is vital to read the signs. Failure to do so will be detrimental to the horse's long-term training. These signs include stopping, going slower, going higher, jumping into trouble, going faster to get finished, and knocking down poles rather than trying to leave them up.

When schooling, if the horse makes a mistake, he should be encouraged to try again and find a different solution. If he continually makes a mistake, you must make him aware of your displeasure at his inability to solve the problem. When the horse succeeds in solving the puzzle and is rewarded— he must really know he is being rewarded—he understands that this is the correct answer. In producing correct answers, the neurological pathways are reinforced with myelin, which makes the messages travel even quicker (see "Create a Learning Pathway," p. 27).

Gymnastic jumping also develops the horse physically, as the correct muscles have to be used to perform the task and, in the process, they are exercised. The questions must initially be simple, and then when they are answered well, they can be made more difficult. Some horses are particularly good at gymnastics, while others need to be educated. As the horse's abil-

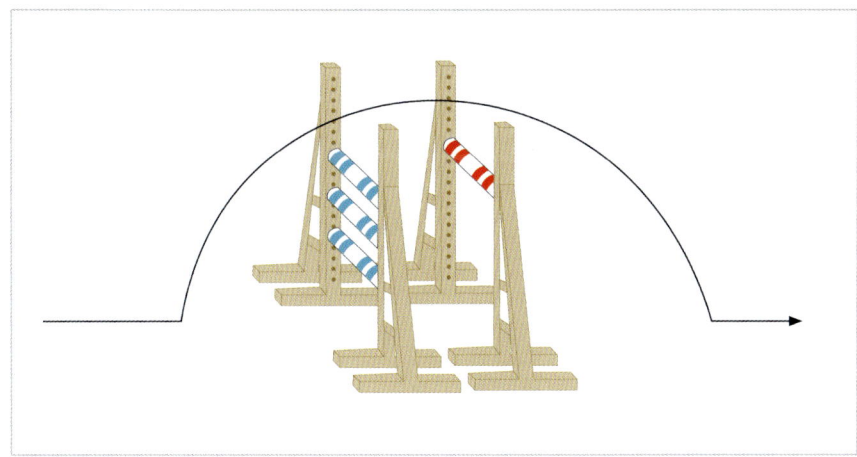

12.12 The highest part of the horse's bascule should come over the highest part of the fence.

12.13 A simple bounce exercise. Note how the horse "looks" at the question he is being asked to solve. In "looking" he is getting ready to ensure his foot-work is correct and that he assesses the next jump.

ily to solve problems gets better, so the complexity of the exercises can be increased.

It is important to ask yourself which part of the jump you want to improve. With all gymnastics, the aim is to produce the highest part of the horse's bascule over the highest point of the jump (fig. 12.12). The person on the ground has to watch how the horse thinks and uses himself to negotiate the fence. The takeoff, in the air and landing must be studied because each phase can be influenced, though maybe not all at the same time. It is important for the person on the ground to watch how the horse's facial expression changes as the questions become more complex.

At the point of takeoff, the horse must look at the jump, taking ownership of the task of jumping, pause momentarily while assessing, and then take off, coming "off" the front of the jump. Stage-managing the "look" is one of the most important parts to this phase (fig. 12.13). By using poles in front of jumps you can increase the "look" element (figs. 12.14 A–D).

Depending on the horse and his way of going, next you can either focus on improving the landing or what he does in the air. Sometimes helping the landing will automatically help the "in the air" part and vice versa. When the horse is asked to look at where he needs to place his feet on landing, you are not only encouraging attention to detail, but also making the distances between jumps easier to ride because the horse will be landing where the course designer intended.

> **Given the correct training and responsibilities, most horses want to jump clear.**

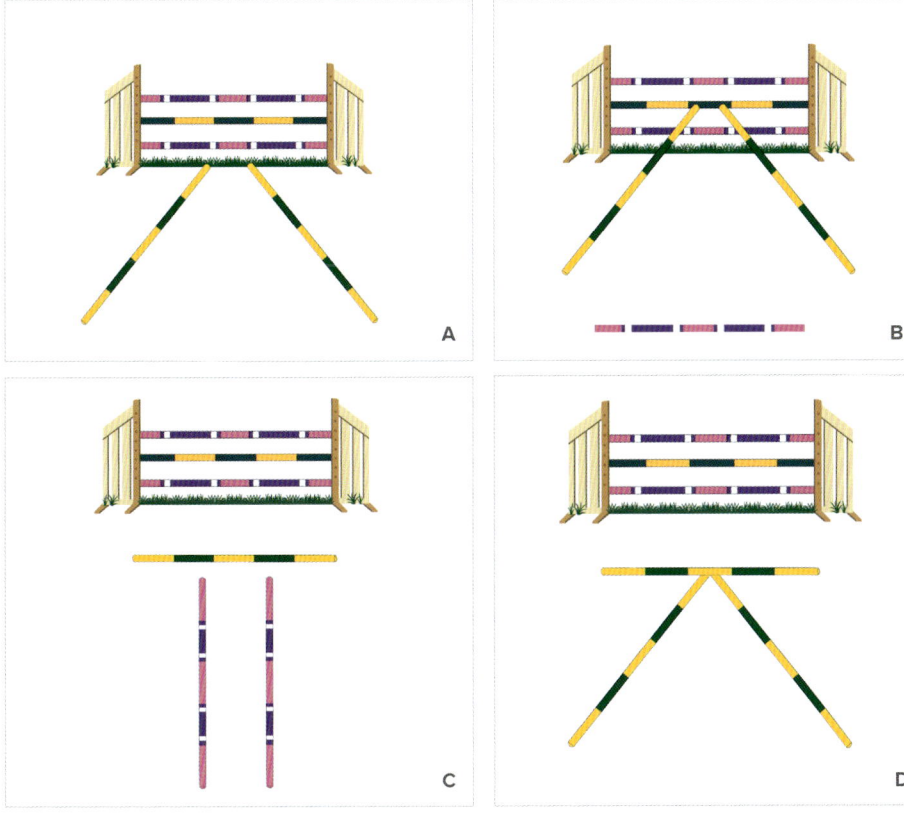

12.14 A–D "V" rails can be used in different ways to help improve the horse's "look" (attention on the fence before him) and focus.

Developing Carefulness

The expression, "Some are, some aren't," is not always true when it comes to care over colored poles. I have known horses that have jumped clear in spite of me and horses that knocked down poles no matter how or by whom they were ridden. I do believe, however, that given the correct training and responsibilities, most horses want to jump clear. When horses are loose schooled, very few knock jumps down; they make some sort of plan about how to get to the other side cleanly. Not all horses have great jumping ability, but most should be able to jump a course of around 3.5 feet (1.10m to 1.15m).

So how do you stand the best chance of producing a horse that takes care over colored poles? By giving him a conscience.

> **As the horse's footwork improves, so his confidence grows and anxiety lessens.**

Schooling is obviously important, but so too is the partnership: knowing who is responsible for what, how to engender ownership—sole and joint—and how each partner should be helping the other to do his or her job (see "The Five Phases of Jumping," p. 115).

Correct schooling encourages horses to make decisions and learn what becomes a good decision. The suppression of the desire to make a decision for fear that it may be wrong is the death knell of good jumping. As the horse is introduced to walking over a pole, a tree root, or a branch, he must be encouraged to pay attention to its presence. Being inattentive is not acceptable—and it is never possible to be over-attentive. To jump or spook at a pole, or to want to avoid a pole, shows an awareness and the beginning of a conscience. This can only be good.

Riders have a responsibility to encourage certain instincts in horses and reward them. When the horse steps cleanly over a pole, he should be rewarded. When he hits a pole, he should be made aware that he was wrong. By making it clear what is acceptable and what is not, the horse starts to make an effort to do the thing that produces a reward. Being consistent with this process produces a mind that makes a habit of trying not to touch poles—a good habit, which then becomes a good instinct.

This can be reinforced by applying the same method over poles on the ground (see chapter 11, p. 106). Horses that try to jump poles and pick up their

Too Much, Too Soon

Any system that has the sole aim of producing horses for sale has spoiled as many animals as it has made. The commercial aspect of producing horses as two-, three-, and four-year-olds means that, inevitably, their training is hurried. To excel at Performance Sales, horses need to show something more than just potential. This can only be achieved through accelerated learning. To reach a particular stage at a given time means that it is not possible to give the horse time to develop at his own pace. This creates gaps in the basic work, which may never be filled and limits progress. These gaps mean that horses can easily be over-faced, and over-facing the mind limits the progress of the body.

This applies to all equestrian disciplines. Let me explain why.

Not every horse is a natural jumper, but every horse can learn to jump well. Riders often tell me that their horse is careless, but more often than not there are pieces of the process missing, which means that the horse has become unable to jump clear.

Horses that struggle to find their balance in canter often have poles down because getting to the jump is tricky. In trying to "help" improve the canter, the rider becomes the distraction. Add a jump into the mix and it all becomes too much.

Fixing the canter is a prerequisite to improving the jump, but you can only layer on jump work when the canter is good enough to remain regular and in some sort of a balance to get to the jump. It need not be perfect, otherwise no one would ever get jumping, but horse and rider must arrive at the fence with something that is satisfactory (for a mark of "6," in dressage-speak—see p. 71). To reach this stage, the horse must listen to the rein aids that are managing his front end and the leg aids that are influencing his back end. This, too, has to be layered onto the other qualities of going forward, and being straight and regular.

Following this logic produces a message that has more chance of being understood. It is also less likely to produce unnecessary glitches that will then need correcting.

feet early tend to be decision-makers. Even though he might be doing something you do not want at that time, he should not be punished. If you repeat the exercise to see if he makes a different decision, it soon becomes obvious whether the horse is a thinker. Changing where he puts his feet is good, even though it may initially produce an incorrect answer. Further repetition will almost certainly result in a different answer that will be more acceptable. You should not be shy with your praise of the horse when he has solved the question. This continues the process of creating a consistent environment for the horse to learn. It is a very sound principle.

Encouraging the development of the correct neurological pathways and producing a thinking horse that is able and willing to take decisions has as much to do with nurture as nature. Certainly, some horses are better at it than others and, like humans, at picking up skills; some find it quickly while others take longer.

As this process happens you also have responsibilities, the greatest one being an unchanged arrival at the obstacle with *no* variables to distract the horse from his problem-solving.

Be conscious about how much help you give, when to do it, and decide whether it is active help or passive support that is required. Jumping is ultimately the horse's job, so you must not do it for him.

Solving Jumping Problems

 How can I stop my horse rushing at fences?

Rushing can happen before and after a fence and there are many reasons for it. The most common include over-riding, uncertainty, fear, and misunderstanding. Many problems that result in rushing before the jump will also produce a running-away response on landing. It is important to try to find the cause before looking for a solution.

An understanding of the task is a good start point. Trotting to the jump, possibly with a placing pole to help arrive in the correct spot, is a useful place to begin. Knowing that the horse understands where to put his feet and what is required of him produces understanding. Developing a canter that remains in balance and isn't held together will always help the arrival. You should ensure you are not stopping him rushing by using too much bit/contact pressure. A short approach off a curve will help prevent this tendency (see "Geometry and Jumping," p. 120).

As the horse's footwork improves, so his confidence grows and anxiety lessens. With a better arrival he is less likely to run away afterward. A proactive landing and getaway should be clear to the horse, giving him a focus of where he is going. His energy will then be channeled on a purpose, which will also help to alleviate rushing.

Turning on landing can make a horse feel unbalanced, but this feeling can also make him want to find a better balance for himself, and so his learning progresses.

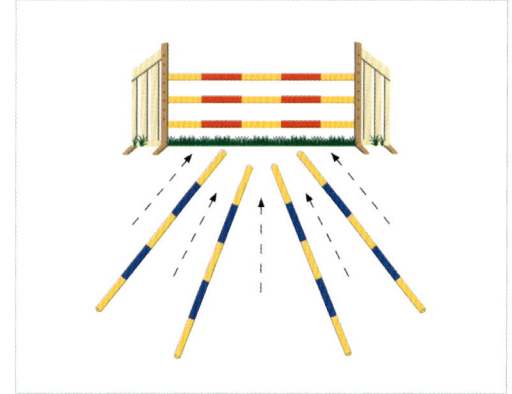

12.15 A & B Guide rails used in this way can help with a horse that drifts as they can improve his focus.

Q **I find it hard to keep my horse on a line. What exercises can I do to improve this?**

A Horses that are distracted often drift, so spend time making sure the horse is listening to your input when you are trying to stay on a line.

Using poles as guide rails can be really useful (figs. 12.15 A & B). It is not necessary to always go to the center of the pole, but instead choose your own line and focus on developing the horse's honesty to that line. This will then improve

your feel in front of a jump. It also encourages the horse to be patient and trust his rider.

 My horse jumps to the left, which makes it hard in related distances. How should I correct this?

 Many horses jump crookedly. The first thing to try and decide is *why* he jumps to the left. Is it his training or his natural tendency? Once you understand why you can try to solve the issue.

Horses that drift naturally are sometimes doing it to give themselves more room. In this case, you must teach him that there is another way to find more room, but also stay straight (see "Mental Gymnastics," p. 128).

When the problem is caused by a deficiency in the training, you can fix it by using guide rails to encourage the horse to straighten.

Often, horses show signs of wanting to jump crookedly when they are reaching the limit of their ability—either naturally or through being hampered by poor schooling.

Choose the Mind, Not the Technique

The very first horse my wife Sue and I owned together was a yearling called Spirit, by the famous eventing sire, Master Spiritus. When I began her education as a rising four-year-old my instincts at the time told me she couldn't jump because of a poor technique. She didn't lift her shoulders, and didn't seem very quick of mind. Or so I thought.

I duly sold her to a good friend of mine, the Irish show jumper, Trevor Coyle. He proceeded to jump her to Grade A and rode her in mini Grands Prix.

One day I asked him, "What did I miss?"

He replied, "She is so careful despite her technique. She would turn a somersault to avoid touching a fence."

It was a good lesson for me to learn: look at the mind, not the technique, and give a horse time.

 My horse hollows in front of a fence. What can I do to encourage him to bascule?

 Most hollow jumps stem from a hollow way of going in front of the fence. A good arrival, with the horse looking at the jump and not being "held off," will allow him to assess the question. Then you can encourage him to look for the landing and so improve the shape he makes in the air.

Making the horse more responsible on takeoff is important. Exercises to help this include building low spreads, double crosses, and having poles on the landing (see "Mental Gymnastics," p. 128).

Q Recently my horse has started throwing in the odd stop. What could be causing this?

A Stopping happens for lots of reasons, but it is seldom badness from the horse. The most likely cause is over-facing him. This can happen in lots of ways: too much jumping too soon, too high a jump, a lack of understanding about how to solve the question, a bad approach, poor quality of gait in front of the jump, or possibly sore feet.

To rectify it you need to retrace the training steps until the horse's mind opens up again. It doesn't matter how small the jump is, but the horse needs to say, "Yes, I can." Then you know you are back on the right track and it is possible to move forward again with the training.

CHAPTER THIRTEEN

Riding in Open Space

In the last 20 years or so, more and more people have become "arena riders," opting to work their horse in the relative "safety" of an enclosed ring rather than venturing out into open spaces and riding over varied terrain and footing. I am very well aware of the reasons for this; not least the rider's uncertainty of letting go and trusting her horse when they do get out into the country.

But horses that spend the majority of their time in arenas need to refresh their natural instincts in order to feel comfortable in the great outdoors. From a coach's perspective this means that when I start thinking about cross-country training I must first look at encouraging riders to allow their horses to be horses and teaching them what they should expect by doing this. Only then can you have a meaningful training session; otherwise too much "school" riding goes with you into the country—to the detriment of good cross-country riding.

Horses have a wonderful awareness of where they are and what they need to do—if they are allowed!

This is not a contradiction to my saying earlier that the fundamental skills of all three disciplines—dressage, show jumping, and eventing—are the same no matter what the discipline. I am merely making the point that cross-country includes many skills not tested in the arena. Some of these skills lie dormant in the horse and may never have been learned by the rider. To truly make the most of the cross-country experience, it is important to rekindle these instincts in the horse and develop the rider's awareness of them.

Cross-country has its dangers and it is the coach and rider's responsibility to mitigate these risks. To show jump in the country and look for a perfect takeoff spot does not always make it safer, nor should riders be overburdened looking for good distances. Some might say otherwise. I would argue that it shows fundamental flaws in the concept of cross-country riding and the training that goes into it. Many of the skills are complementary, but many are unique to riding over solid fences outdoors.

Crossing the country is not a refined science; to do it well requires two minds and their instincts. Horses have a wonderful awareness of where they are and what they need to do—if they are allowed!

Cross-country riding is about being in a trusting partnership: *two individuals, each fully understanding their role, working for a common cause.* It is not fair to ask a horse to jump something that he has not been taught in training. He must be allowed to develop the skills he will be asked to demonstrate when competing.

By the same token, riders need to do their bit. Many skills require practice: the change in balance, the variation in speed, judgment of speed, and how to ride the terrain. The ability to change the whip from hand to hand as required, being able to shorten the reins after a drop before a narrow jump, and moving the horse onto a chosen line. It is irresponsible of riders not to have honed these skills and have ingrained them as second nature.

➤ Having the stick in the wrong hand and running out at a corner jump is irresponsible!

➤ Traveling downhill to a narrow jump while grappling with long, unknotted reins and running out is irresponsible!

In training, horses need to know they are being asked to take an interest and not just do what the rider instructs. Once involved, it is possible to run to a fence without needing to arrive perfectly, as the horse that makes a decision will always be "right enough." This is a win-win situation: two minds, solving problems, and being able to beat the clock because of the seamless join between galloping and jumping. *This* is cross-country.

Roles and Responsibilities

Only once you are used to riding outside and have got your horse comfortable with the ground conditions can training begin. Starting before this happens can cause problems, and a bad experience over solid jumps can leave a lasting impression.

> **The ability to ride and be comfortable working outside the arena is a major part of everyone's training.**

The ability to ride and be comfortable working outside the arena is a major part of everyone's training. If a combination is accustomed to the footing, is secure in the balance, and has control of the line and the adjustment of pace, cross-country schooling will start in a good place.

There are a few similarities between training for show jumping and cross-country, namely *line* and *pace* (see p. 24). These two variables are your responsibility. The horse does the jumping.

The dividing up of responsibilities is a subject I have already explored (see "Five Phases of Jumping," p. 115), but you now need to understand how it happens cross-country. Much depends on the level of education of the partnership. In the early stages, it is important to allow time for both you and

Education vs. Instinct

In the days when hunting was the playground for eventers, horses learned to look after themselves. They honed the crucial skills for safely crossing the country: speed of thought, co-ordination, spatial awareness, and self-preservation.

Horses that are willful often make great decisions, but with more and more emphasis being placed on dressage and show jumping, they have fewer opportunities to do this. The more a horse allows himself to be ridden, the more the rider feels obliged to do the riding, and in doing so, takes over the decision-making.

It is not that today's horses are incapable of acting to "instinct training," it's just they are not allowed to develop these skills. It is the rider's responsibility to create opportunities that allow them to do this.

the horse to assimilate and understand the question. This means that the lines taken need to give a clear or reasonably clear view of the jump, and the speed of the gait is likely to be slower to allow the horse time to think. As good answers become the norm and the partnership develops confidence in its decision-making, so the lines can be tightened and the speed increased. Coaching this skill is both fun and interesting, as watching partnerships develop at different speeds requires a flexible plan.

Natural Instincts

Taking horses into a field or open space ignites a number of natural instincts that tend to be dormant in the arena. These include:

➤ A heightened sense of awareness of the surroundings.

➤ The availability of space to flee if need be.

➤ Terrain that requires more care to remain in balance.

➤ An understanding of how to gallop.

Often riders become unsure or frightened about how to deal with the "new" horse they experience. This means that spending more time getting the partnership used to the feelings of "life on grass" can only be a good thing. Too much time is spent in the arena anyway.

Let us look in more detail of some of the differences.

➤ A horse that is more aware of his surroundings is something all riders feel when they leave the confines of the arena. Horses can be different anywhere away from home or in a different environment, but rather than saying, "He won't settle today," "He's rather lit up," or "She's in season," it is more helpful to know what is the norm away from home and work out how to deal with it. It may take a while, require a lot of thought, and challenge your skills, but this is all part of the rich tapestry of horsemanship. Using simple tasks and exercises that the partnership knows well will help bring the horse and rider's attention back into focus.

➤ With more space a horse will often produce bigger and more open gaits. How often people have said, "Wow, what a trot," "Gosh he can gallop," as they watch a horse playing in the field. This openness of gait can be difficult to contain or direct, especially if you are caught unaware. Some people resort to stronger bits as a solution, but we know that more problems are created than solved by going down this path (see "Bitting," p. 150). The solution lies in riders acquainting themselves with—and not being intimidated by—the feeling of extra power and being able to guide it into something constructive.

➤ Terrain and footing is a more important subject than people imagine (see "No Arena? No Problem," p. 97). A horse's balance changes when he is not on a predictable surface. He needs to get used to this unpredictability and manage himself accordingly. In the wild he does this instinctively and you must always allow this instinct to be present as this is a big part of his stability. Getting used to going up and down hills, crossing undulating ground and uncertain terrain is the cross-country horse's bread and butter. His confidence in negotiating this type of ground improves his ability to focus on the jumps and the issues in store for him. Rider support is helpful, but it must not be dictatorial. Horses need to learn to look after themselves.

➤ Horses are not natural gallopers, they are natural sprinters. The two things are different. They sprint to get away from danger, but not all horses find the managed, controlled speed of galloping easy. This is a skill you must teach, just as you teach them to accept and be between your aids in the other three gaits. This should begin with riding a controlled canter/gallop of around 350 meters per minute increasing to 400mpm, and gradually up to 500mpm. The horse needs time to become accustomed to being in a balance, between the aids and attentive to them. This way he will conserve energy. This is an important skill for cross-country horses to learn and time should be spent instilling this. The rewards are plentiful.

Why Temperament Matters

It is important to remember that riders will ride according to their own characteristics. Horses also have individual traits as part of their character. Some are cautious, some foolhardy, some strong-willed, others fragile. Most have a left or right bias. To provide the best guidance, I need to recognize a partnership's individual traits—good and bad—and tailor my advice accordingly. Deciding whose problem it is needs careful thought.

The Rider

➤ The cautious rider may feel more comfortable with a horse that is good at making decisions.

➤ The foolhardy rider might find this horse becomes too bold with her.

➤ As humans we all have a bias to right or left; this needs to be recognized.

➤ The strong-willed rider may well be good with a timid horse.

➤ Some riders like horses that take a hold, others do not.

The Horse

The same applies to the horse: He can be naturally brave or very cautious. He might show a preference for right or left and be mostly confident with the challenges that going cross-country pose: hidden

Useful Cross-Country Start Points

When you run into trouble cross-country, try reverting to one or more of the following start points:

➤ Slow down and give the horse time to think.

➤ Do not take decisions away from him.

➤ Take an easy route to recover his confidence.

➤ Repeat what was done last time in training.

landings, jumping into water, holding lines, and negotiating ditches. In contrast, the horse that lacks confidence or experience can be over-careful with his jump, stop, run out, drift, over-jump, or rush. When any of these signs appear it is important that the training steps are retraced to a suitable start point (see "Start Point," p. 69). It is up to you and your coach to identify where that might be, so the training can recommence from a point of security.

Rider Position

This is a subject that is constantly under discussion and experts everywhere have different views. But there is common ground—every good rider is in balance. Without balance, the communication, efficiency, and security are diminished.

First, remind yourself about the two ends of the scale: the dressage rider's position and the jockey's position. Why are they so different?

It is all to do with the center of balance of the partnership. Dressage riders strive to move their center of balance backward to lighten the fore-hand and so position themselves accordingly, while jockeys try to position themselves as far forward as they can because the speed and longer stride of a racehorse in full gallop takes their center of balance there.

> **Whatever the position, every good rider is in balance.**

Stirrup lengths for a show jumper can be four to six holes shorter than that of a dressage rider, while for cross-country, irons can be shortened two or three holes again from the show-jumping length. Much depends on the shape and biomechanics of the individual rider, her comfort of body and mind, and the saddle and how it fits.

There is not one position that fits all cross-country, and it is not sensible to suggest this is the case. There are, however, certain principles of cross-country riding that always need to be considered:

➤ Security of the lower leg.

➤ Angle of the upper leg.

➤ Weight on the stirrup.

> Upper body above foot position.

> Core weight above foot position.

> Seat close to the saddle.

> Use of a suitable saddle.

Take a look at good examples of jumper rider positions (figs. 13.1 A & B). The point to note is the security of the leg position, which allows for good balance. The leg remains underneath the rider's body weight. As jumps get bigger, there tends to be a little more upper-body movement to stay with the horse.

13.1 A & B Top show jumper Beezie Madden shows an excellent position over a fence in A. She says, "The security of the lower leg is required for balance and communication, (both qualities) essential for high performance." Sarah Ballou, a pupil of mine, is being rather "enthusiastic" with her upper body in B, but like Beezie, she demonstrates a very secure lower leg position.

There are three positions used when riding cross-country (figs. 13.2 A–C). All adhere to the principles listed earlier:

➤ The closed seat.

➤ The light seat.

➤ The forward seat.

➤ (Some would also say there is a fourth: the "Oh @!#$" seat!)

Every rider functions in a different way, so coaches should spend time watching and exploring individual needs, and explaining and demonstrating how each individual should "condition" herself. Once established, the seat then requires practice to allow you to master the balance until it becomes

13.2 A–C These riders are in different positions, but all demonstrate a secure leg position that's underneath their body weight. The first rider demonstrates a closed seat in front of a jump (A). The second shows a well-balanced, light seat (B). Finally, we see a forward seat (C).

comfortable and ultimately, second nature. Practicing off a horse can help develop the core strength necessary to hold the position without it appearing forced or unnatural (fig. 13.3).

When practiced on the ground, you can completely focus on what is needed to make the position happen. This can be done in front of a long mirror. Experimenting with going between positions helps develop your own neurological pathways that need to be exercised. It may feel strange to start with, but the more often it is done, the easier it becomes.

13.3 Another good example of an excellent seat and lower-leg position.

You should be careful about trying to copy your heroes or other jockeys you admire. It is the champions' instincts and reactions that make them who they are. Philip Dutton and Izzy Taylor (fig. 13.4) are both brilliant cross-country riders, but both ride in very different ways that take account of their shape and size. It is important to look at the skills top riders display and try and emulate their good points, but individuals should find a style and balance that suits them.

13.4 **British eventer Izzy Taylor demonstrating exceptional balance over a large oxer.**

A Bit of an Issue

We all know that times have changed in equestrian sport and continue to do so. Change in itself is not necessarily a bad thing—it can be for the better—but it is also important to reflect on this change from time to time, otherwise it is easy for certain practices to become adopted and quickly accepted as being correct when the signs are in fact the opposite.

Bits and their uses fall into this category. It is a subject that I have been vocal about for years. I have written articles and received a lot of support for my views. It is an issue that applies to all equestrian disciplines, although the most serious safety concerns are inevitably linked with cross-country riding.

The issues tend to be the same, although they manifest in different ways in different disciplines, as I will explain later.

I first noticed the desire to achieve greater control when the minimum weight restriction was removed from the eventing cross-country phase in 1998 (previously all horses had to carry 165lbs (75kg), made up with lead weight if necessary, for the cross-country phase). At the same time, courses started becoming more technical. These two changes brought control into focus as lighter riders were now riding big, "scopey" horses, and they needed better control to negotiate the more technical courses. The short fix was to find a bit that offered more control.

A similar thing happened in show jumping. Bigger jumping horses were introduced—they were not necessarily better or more careful, they just had bigger jumps. Courses became more technical, so there became a need to control these horses.

In dressage, the desire for control has taken a different route. While there have been adaptations to the snaffle and double bridles, these two pieces of tack have remained a constant. Crank nosebands and hyperflexion have become the focus.

When it comes to bits there has always been a fashion, a "must have," a "follow the trend." Bit manufacturers see opportunities in the market and take them, convincing the uninitiated that a certain bit will make all the difference because it is "kinder to the horse" or "more natural."

> When it comes to bitting, it is important for us all to seek a moral common ground.

Bitting to gain control produces problems for everyone, from the happy hacker to the upper level rider. Coaches must feel like they are swimming against a tide when they advocate correct acceptance and understanding of the rider's aids, and instead, see three-rings, pulleys, and big hunks of metal. The welfare and integrity of the horse remain paramount, but, at times, it seems this has been replaced by the need for control at all costs.

When double bridles were permitted in the dressage phase of eventing, riders saw this as an opportunity to gain the control they felt they were missing in a snaffle. Thank goodness this trend has been identified and rule changes seem to be coming in to rectify this. In show jumping it appears that riders will resort to anything in order to gain control, provided it is within the rules.

Every discipline has its own requirements and some would say that it is not possible to draw comparisons. But I think there are similarities and that it is important for us all to seek a moral common ground.

We all want a nice riding horse: one that goes, stops, and turns on request. When asked to jump, we want the horse to know what to do. When asked to gallop, we don't want him to run away. In dressage, the "Carl Hester effect" has changed the face of the discipline throughout the world. To watch and listen to this brilliant horseman should be a must for all riders. In time, the ethical way of training that Carl so inspires will filter right through the sport at all levels.

Does the end justify the means? No, of course not, but we need to be careful to supervise that it does not. At this year's Junior and Young Rider European Championships for all disciplines, I was able to watch each discipline warm up for their respective classes; because of the age grouping most riders had trainers. Indeed that's why I was there. I was struck by the difficulty the stewards have in enforcing the rules. Not so much when they are clearly defined (as in show jumping), but more so the interpretation of the rules in the dressage warm-up. Each rider had a headset on and was being instructed by her trainer. In many cases, it amounted to "supervised bullying" of the horse with a high degree of "mental cruelty"—always on the edge of the rules and their interpretation. Hyperflexion, excessive use of spur and or whip, seeking "false paces" in place of correct and ethical schooling.

Classical principles dating to Xenophon some 2400 years ago should still be upheld today:

1 That the horse should be allowed to develop naturally.

2 That force should not be used.

3 That the result should be beautiful and beautifully easy to watch.

In show jumping, jumping clear is the aim. The issue of making horses careful is, and always will be, part of the sport. The ethics of how this is achieved is open to much debate. Bits and bitting can be a part of this.

But it is for eventing that I have my main concern with the misuse of bits. In dressage and show jumping there are undoubtedly issues, but cross-country there is far more danger lurking.

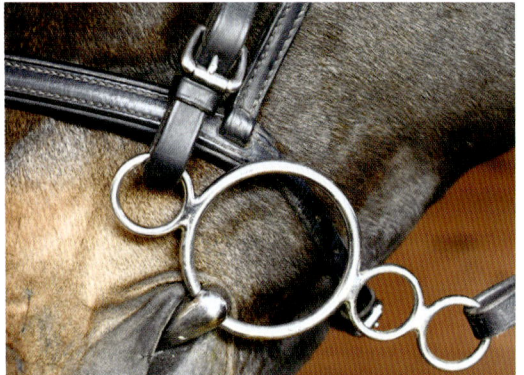

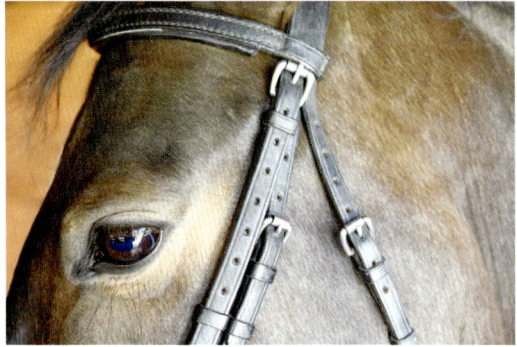

13.5 A & B A three-ring bit, which is almost always fitted on the last hole because the cheek pieces are too long. With no wrinkles at the lip (not shown) and the bit at full rotation it now has the same action as a snaffle. So why not start with a snaffle?

"Fake" Control

Horses are not natural gallopers. Their instinct allows them to sprint, but they must be taught to gallop, just as they are taught to walk, trot, and canter. To perform in all gaits in harmony and control should be every rider's aim. Without this harmony and understanding, we open a Pandora's box of possible problems.

Asking a horse to gallop at Preliminary (US) or Novice (UK) cross-country speed of 520mpm before he is comfortable with a fast canter (350–400mpm) has every chance of triggering his natural response of "run." The moment speed becomes a conditioned response to the rider shortening her stirrups and getting into an open space, the rider feels the need to control it. Now problems arise and the perception is that brakes are needed.

The range of bits and gadgets is endless. Some of the most popular are:

➤ The three-ring or bubble bit (figs. 13.5 A & B).

➤ The elevator (fig. 13.6).

➤ Rings and pulley reins in various forms.

➤ Curb chains—excessively tight.

Every one of these is a potential disaster waiting to happen!

The aim of flatwork training is to produce a nice riding horse for all occasions. As the topline is rounded to encourage the horse "through" from leg to hand, an acceptance and understanding of the aid is produced. This harmony must also be present cross-country.

The bits I have listed above, and others like them, have an action that

13.6 A bit like the elevator on this horse can cause a horse to hollow and produce an uncomfortable jump.

encourages hollowness in the horse's way of going that is detrimental both on the flat and over fences. Not every horse has a natural bascule over a jump—and we should make every effort to work with what the horse is given and encourage him to *buy in* to what he has to do to jump. But by using bits that encourage an incorrect way of going, we create many problems for ourselves and the horse:

➤ The jaw shows resistance.

➤ The head comes up.

➤ The neck goes hollow.

➤ The shoulders become blocked.

Follow the Danes

It is interesting that Denmark only allows snaffles and pelhams in the sport of eventing. The logic is driven by a belief that these two "families" of bits are more likely to promote better riding and educated horses. Food for thought. I would like more countries to follow Denmark's example.

- The steering becomes delayed and unresponsive.

- The back becomes less "through."

- The rider stops using her legs for fear of more speed.

- The horse's hind legs are less engaged.

- The rider's hands become the dominant aid.

And so it goes on.

The problems that occur when hollowness appears can manifest in different ways:

- Lack of roundness to a jump.

- Dragging of hind legs (causing poles to fall down behind).

- Tight shoulders (causing more poles down in front).

- Tight shoulders (causing more chance of hitting solid fences).

- More stand-offs or long spots.

- More speed, less impulsion.

> **The harmony we expect to achieve on the flat must also be present cross-country.**

Spend a day watching cross-country and you will see some unsightly pictures. Look more closely and there is also a trend: most of the ugly sights are control issues. Look more closely and you will see these control issues will also have a bit issue.

Course designers cannot make the jumping phases of eventing higher or wider in their effort to separate competitors, so they have had to use their imagination to test the control of horse and rider. Course designers explore the concepts of the control of line and pace, the control of accuracy, and the riders' training of their horse in answering this control.

Coaching riders and horses to meet these challenges of control requires skill, but there is a perception that this increase in skill is a euphemism for more control. More control can come from an improvement in the way the partnership works together, or it can be tack-induced. The latter is a shortcut. This is not to say that a change in tack can never make a difference for the better, but it is important to know how to retain the good qualities when in control and not to just "be in control"! There is too much of the latter.

A lot of our everyday problems are directly attributable to bits and bitting. Moreover, only a handful of top riders are skilled enough to "cope" with the issues created by bitting, leaving the rest to struggle with the consequences of these issues.

Straightness and Sensitivity

Bitting can also cause straightness issues. As the course builder tests honesty and accuracy at arrowheads, corners, and offset lines, so the need to hold a line becomes vital. Bits that act on the lips tend have a delayed response, so correcting a drift or possible runout when the horse loses the line risks 20 penalties.

A bit that is too severe tests the rider's sensitivity in its use when holding lines—too much or too little pressure can result in an unwanted answer.

> **"More bit" seldom helps.**

The use of rings and pulleys that lie close to the horse's skin can also trigger problems. Any rope crossing skin over bone will result in the skin losing its sensitivity. This tends to happen in just a few minutes with prolonged pressure. Try it on your own wrist and then imagine what it might feel like after a period of prolonged pressure (fig. 13.7). When riding in an arena, a horse seldom goes fast enough or keeps going long enough for this to happen, therefore, the issue of desensitization is irrelevant. But cross-country, this pressure can be on the horse's face for a much longer period of time, and he is going much faster, so desensitization can occur as early as three or four minutes into the course. The result is a horse with a diminished response, or one that runs from the pain by running through the hand or bridle.

Often, the horse that goes in the strongest bits will have issues that are longstanding and not easy to correct. He tends to be the one that makes a bid for the jump. In attempting to gain "control" of this type of horse, the rider can

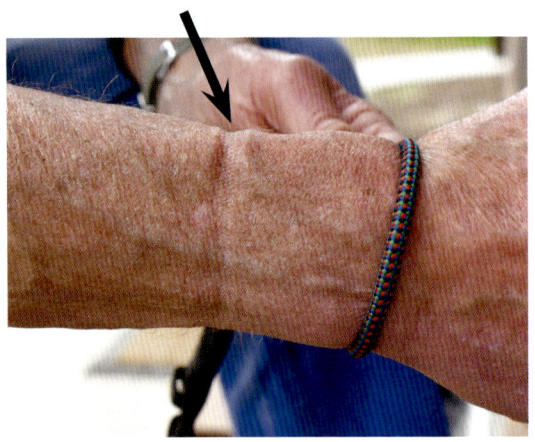

13.7 Like the effect this rope has had on my wrist, prolonged pressure from ropes across the nose and or the lower jaw are likely to cause a desensitization of the area.

get drawn into an ever-increasing desensitization of the places a bit acts upon and down a rocky road of increasingly severe bits.

Reeducating an older, more conditioned horse is much harder than dealing with an animal that is simply young and exuberant. To reawaken an older horse's senses is a task for experts, and sometimes, even for them, it is not possible. "More bit" seldom helps. A horse's mind and body becomes insensitive to discomfort and pain.

I have judged eventing at the two-star level and seen 50 percent of the horses doing dressage in a double bridle. When this happens, alarm bells ring! Intermediate horses should not need double bridles. Their use is an attempt to cover up educational faults or deficiencies. Of the 50 percent, most then went cross-country in bits other than a snaffle. Around 25 percent had falls, which resulted in a number of trips to the hospital.

You may think I am being alarmist, but I believe that coaches and riders have a responsibility to properly educate horses to mitigate the risks as much as possible. Cross-country riding should be about having fun, but it is also important to think about preserving the future of the sport. The right education is the only way to avoid this bit epidemic becoming even more of a safety hazard. We need to take time to educate young horses, to teach them how to canter and gallop by happily accepting and understanding the aids from leg to hand. Above all, though, we need to encourage them to look after themselves when jumping.

Solving Cross-Country Problems

Problems over solid fences are rarely fixed with "Band-Aid" solutions. Identifying the root of the issue is the place to start.

Every level of competition asks similar questions; the only things that change are the dimensions of the obstacles, the speed the questions come

When Cross-Country Becomes Dangerous

Good cross-country horses look, think, and react. To the rider who says, "He'll jump anything," I reply, "That's not always a good thing."

To produce a suitable canter or gallop, the horse must allow himself to be balanced by accepting the rider's leg aids. These aids should engage the hind end in a way that doesn't produce speed, but encourages the horse to accept the contact and the resulting adjustment to speed in a round and rideable way. Failure to do this makes it difficult for the horse to see, assess, and take responsibility for his part in the jump.

Imagine a car with its accelerator stuck on and the brake as the only regulator of speed. The driver would survive for a short time but very soon the brakes would overheat and fail. This is what happens to over-bitted horses—it is called "running through the bridle"—and it can have frightening results.

Hollowness over solid fences is a problem in itself, but add in a drop behind and safety becomes a very real issue. When the horse is unable to see what he has to do until the last second, he will not be able to react quickly enough to stay safe. Furthermore, the way the horse is likely to hit the fence will be with his forelegs above the knee. This is the type of impact that often causes a rotational fall or a fall on landing as the horse is unable to get his undercarriage under control.

There is an indisputable link between bitting and falls. As the rider endeavors to regain control and balance in front of a fence, the horse inverts and so the ability to ride from the leg to the rein diminishes. The takeoff becomes uncertain, spreads become a lottery, distances in combinations become short, and the "out" element becomes very chancy. A blow on the horse's forearm could be the result, and with it, the risk of a serious fall.

up, and the terrain they appear on. They are a test of the rider's homework and the horse's ability to answer the questions asked of them.

It is not the aim of course designers to find fault, but not every rider or every horse is a top performer. Sometimes, a partnership will struggle when they have reached the limit of their ability. Sometimes one or other, or both parties, are over-faced. At other times, problems occur that are neither the rider nor the horse's fault. On the way up there may also be blips to progressive training, which can highlight the need to do more of something specific: riders (and coaches) need to be honest with themselves to identify this need and give time to its correction.

Horses and riders grow in confidence at different rates, and like a good marriage, partnerships depend on one another in different percentages with each one making up for the other's deficiencies. Rider and coach need to be observant in identifying the signs because the horse can only tell us by his actions. Horses tend to be predictable and when you train them, you need to be mindful of this. What they look at, which way they drift, what makes them over- or under-jump, what they like doing, and so on.

> **Horses and riders grow in confidence at different rates.**

The nearer to the limit of the partnership's ability you go, the more these idiosyncrasies appear. Some may be ironed out with schooling, but in reality, they will always act as a limiting factor.

 My horse has always been suspicious of ditches—particularly trakehners. What can I do?

A Horses need not fear ditches if careful work is done in the beginning. If you inherit a problem horse, then retrace the training and be diligent in solving the anxiety. Allowing your horse to stand and look into a really small ditch and then asking him to walk over it is a good start.

Observe how your horse jumps a small ditch: The horses that jump up and over are the good ditch jumpers; the ones that creep low and get over are not so good. Knowing which category a horse falls into will be important as the ditches get wider because every horse will view the challenge differently. You must include familiarization with "small holes in the ground," because the horse that is accustomed to ditches of all shapes and sizes will have less difficulty with the bigger trakehners than the horse that is still looking into the ditch when there is a log on top to jump.

A really solid foundation is critical to ditches, trakehners, or a surprise approach. The horse must say "Yes" before he considers "Maybe."

Q **My horse is generally bold, except when he can't see where he is going to land. How can I make him more confident?**

A Every aspect of teaching is based on encouraging the horse to look and *buy in* to the question. The horse needs to learn to look and assess for himself, and in doing so, he will begin to work out what he needs to do in order to land carefully and safely. The "look" and jump timing is important to focus on with this type of horse (see p. 130). It must be quick enough so he retains the momentum and doesn't lose the will to try, but slow enough so he can see that it is okay.

The horse that takes off regardless, without looking for the landing, needs retraining—or no riding cross-country at all!

Constant repetition over small, blind-landing jumps will build trust and confidence in what you ask. This, in turn, will build the horse's own self-confidence to give a jump a try.

Q **What should I think about when jumping into and out of water?**

A Start by separating the jump questions. The horse must get used to water on its own and be thoroughly comfortable with it before you add another layer to the question. It is worth remembering that asking a horse to jump into a place where he is unsure of his footing goes against his instincts—in the wild, this is the place where predators lurk.

Spend time getting the horse used to going in and out of the water before adding an in-and-out over very small fences, so that you teach him not to over-jump. When the fences get bigger, he is more likely to go because he is not too busy looking at the water.

Jumping *out* of water generally causes less trouble as you are returning to dry land. The only real issue is not to over-ride as the predictability of distance alters due to the drag of the water.

Q **My coach is always telling me to watch my balance going down drops. Why is this?**

A As with blind landings, horses have to look where they are going and plan how they are going to negotiate the mechanics of the question. Your balance and control of the reins will greatly improve the experience a horse has when negotiating these kinds of obstacles. When you are able to give him a good ride and make him feel confident and comfortable, he will be happy to do it again and again. Staying in the middle of the horse is key to the balance of the partnership (figs. 13.8 A–C).

Q **I have always disliked riding corners and worry my horse is going to run out. What should I be focusing on?**

A Why do you ride the centerline in a dressage test? To see if you can. If you can, you have more chance of jumping a corner successfully because you have proved you can hold a line—*that* is the test.

Horses and riders need to be honest to a line and all your training must focus on this concept. Without honesty, jumping a corner becomes uncertain. Add to this a horse's natural inclination to drift right or left, and the rider's right- or left-handedness, and you can see why there is scope for disaster. So, homework must be done to remove any issues that arise—or better still, do not let them appear in the first place.

13.8 A–C Remove the horse, and the rider stays in balance: these riders demonstrate a very good position when jumping drops of various types.

13.9 A useful setup to help with corners: jumping the arms of the corner first is a good test of honesty to the line. Having successfully completed this, going between the parallel guide poles to the corner will feel easy.

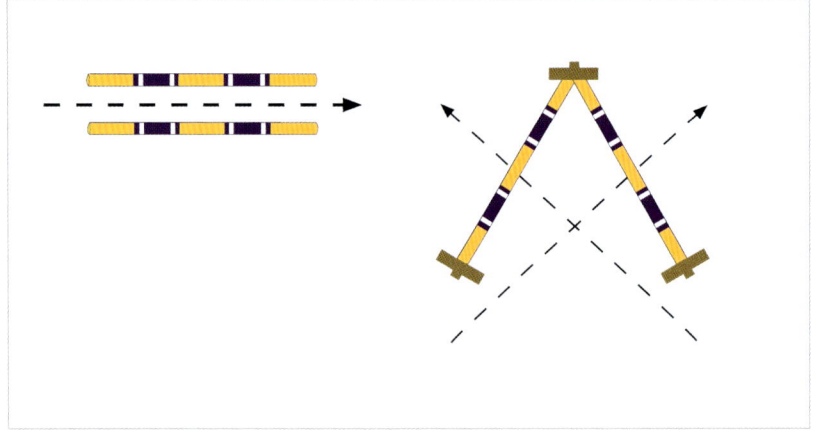

Use guide rails, practice on both reins over small corners, and become thoroughly competent jumping off short strides and off longer, more forward strides. Your horse will then become more trusting and honest with you and himself (fig. 13.9).

Q **Are skinnies more difficult for horses to "read" than corners?**

A Everything I have said about corners applies equally to skinnies or narrows. The difference is that "escape" routes for the horse are easier to find, so he must never be shown them—or if they are already in his mind they must be removed as far as possible.

When horses learn good things they normally try to offer good things. Remember what I said earlier about reaching your limit: the higher the skinny, the narrower it looks, so the more honesty is challenged. *That* is the test.

CHAPTER FOURTEEN

At the Competition

For many riders, competing is the aim. I enjoy training, but I also love putting it all into practice at a competition. How the planning and management of competition days is undertaken will directly affect the rider's enjoyment, stress levels, and ultimately, of course, the result.

Time should be taken to think through the whole process, engaging all of the team. As well as working out a schedule for the day, there are other questions that need addressing: Who will look after the horses left at home? Is there food when everyone gets home late? What will happen to the dog? Thinking things through well in advance will pay dividends as it allows you to focus on the task in hand without being distracted.

Course-Walking

Why do you need to walk the course? This may sound like a silly question, but it is an important one for everyone to ask before setting off.

Some course-walks are for fun, others are very serious. Whether it is a show jumping or a cross-country course walk, the importance of understanding what needs to be achieved cannot be overstated. A celebrity-led course walk at a major event can be educational and entertaining, but a rider who is setting out on the third and final course-walk at a major event will have a very different mindset.

Riders must know their own strengths and limitations as well as those of their horse.

We walk the course to:

➤ Ascertain the way.

➤ Understand the questions.

➤ Think about how these relate to us.

➤ Determine the ground conditions.

➤ Become comfortable with the test.

Walking the Cross-Country

At a one-day event, one cross-country course walk is usually sufficient, but riders should be aiming for at least three walks at a three-day event.

➤ The first walk is to find the way.

➤ The second time is to dissect every question into the minutest detail, looking at all the options available, also being aware of the "What if" scenario.

➤ Third time is to go firm on Plan A, but also ensure Plans B, C, and D are formed.

There are many variables to jumping a clear round. It is important to understand these variables so they can be practiced and used to your advantage.

On every course walk you need to try to get into the mind of the course designer: What is the rider being asked? What are the questions that need answering? How does this fence relate to the last one and the one that follows? Is the designer preparing the rider for something later on? What will the horse think of this?

The last of these is particularly important. Riders must know their own strengths and limitations as well as those of their horse. What does he do when he is fresh? Tired? How fit is he? How honest is he?

Then there are external factors to consider: Do the ground conditions suit the horse? What difference does this make as to how and where will it be best to jump? What are the distractions, other than the fences, and how will the horse react to them? Failure to take in account all these variables will undoubtedly lead to a problem.

Often, as riders walk toward a jump, they are drawn toward a particular route. It is important to be aware of this feeling but not to commit to it until the third walk. The second walk is for looking at every scenario there could possibly be, including the "What if" scenario. This is not a negative thought process; it is positive planning. If Plan A doesn't happen, you must be quick to react to avoid further penalty or time issues. Taking pictures or drawing diagrams can be a useful exercise.

The third and final walk is the time for you to walk it as you want to ride it. You may find that your first instinct was right and that you are still drawn to the first route you saw, but you have followed a process and considered everything.

Having done all the walking, the next thing is to visualize. Find somewhere quiet, close your eyes, and "ride" the course. Go through every fence, turn, dip, hill, and reference point. Helping the mind ride it with a positive outcome reinforces the neurological pathways of going and doing it.

Walking the Show Jumping Course

Course designers tend not to play tricks; they require you to follow a line in a good canter and allow the horse to jump the obstacle when he gets there. They not only test if riders can negotiate the jumps, but whether they can ride the lines the way they are designed to be ridden. Encouraging riders to use the space after every fence is very much part of the course designer's plan. Using it badly or thoughtlessly leads to sloppy riding and possible time faults. It is, after all, the approach to the next fence and it is important that it has a good beginning.

Course designers set tests that are able to be solved by most horses, but not all horses have the same canter, mind, state of schooling, rider, or partnership with that rider. Consequently, there are many variables to jumping a clear round. It is important to understand these variables so they can be practiced and used to your advantage.

The number one rule of serious course-walking is to walk without distractions. This is not a time to be holding hands, fiddling with phones, or have the family tag along offering words of wisdom when they are not wanted. Look around and get a feel for the ground. Begin from the warm-up area, having already established how the warm-up system operates. How and where do you get into the ring? How will this impact on the timing of your final practice fence?

Once in the ring, you have 45 seconds after the bell goes to start. This is valuable time, so it needs to be used wisely. There are times when it goes quickly and other times when it feels like there is all the time in the world. It is

The Three Bucket System

Riding cross-country is all about the management of certain qualities. I like to think of it as having three buckets containing different things: energy, honesty, and time (fig. 14.1). Your aim is not to empty any of them before the finish.

Energy

It seems obvious that the rider must have energy throughout the course, but it is a finite resource and it needs looking after. There are many draws on a horse's energy supply including ground, speed, taking alternative routes, rebalances, acceleration, size of obstacles, turns, and how competitive the rider wants to be.

14.1 The Three Bucket System: How to manage cross-country qualities.

Honesty

The horse has to want to help and find solutions to the questions, but no matter how well trained he is, or how purposefully you set out on the course, situations occur where the horse's honesty is tested. The more you question and ask the horse to prove his honesty the more he may be found wanting. A horse that is tired, has lost a bit of confidence, is asked one question too many, or is being over-faced, is less likely to come up with the right answers. When this

important to have a plan for these 45 seconds. How do you get to fence one? Where are the start markers and time gate? Stay away from them! It is *so* easy to go through them by accident and start the clock. Olympic gold medals have been lost for this very thing. You don't want it to happen to you.

It is worth remembering that every jump is related, so it should be treated as such. Look from one fence to the next, and walk the exact line that the course designer will have walked and measured (fig. 14.2). The lines you choose need to take into account the individual horse and how he jumps and travels between fences.

happens on course the chances of finishing clear are significantly reduced.

Time

To be competitive it is necessary to manage time. Time faults can be expensive and even finishing a fraction over the optimum can mean a drop down the leaderboard. Every second lost early on becomes harder to recover the farther the round progresses. When walking the course it is important to identify places that are a greater draw on time—where there are technical combinations or difficult terrain—and places where it may be possible to make up valuable seconds. Energy and honesty place demands on time management, and when these resources run low, it becomes harder to recover lost time. Putting time in the bank early on may use up energy, which then challenges honesty later on in the course.

Throughout the course you will be dipping into each bucket. It becomes a tradeoff: take an alternative on course and lose time and energy but recover honesty, or take the bold option and dip into the honesty bucket but save time. Maintaining a balance throughout the course becomes the challenge.

There has to be a constant discussion with the horse and a reevaluation of how he feels. Remember, the horse does not know the demands of the course, so it is up to you to weigh up how these three resources are used. To run out of energy or honesty may have serious consequences; to run out of time means being non-competitive.

14.2 When walking the course remember that every fence is related, and walk the exact line the course designer has set.

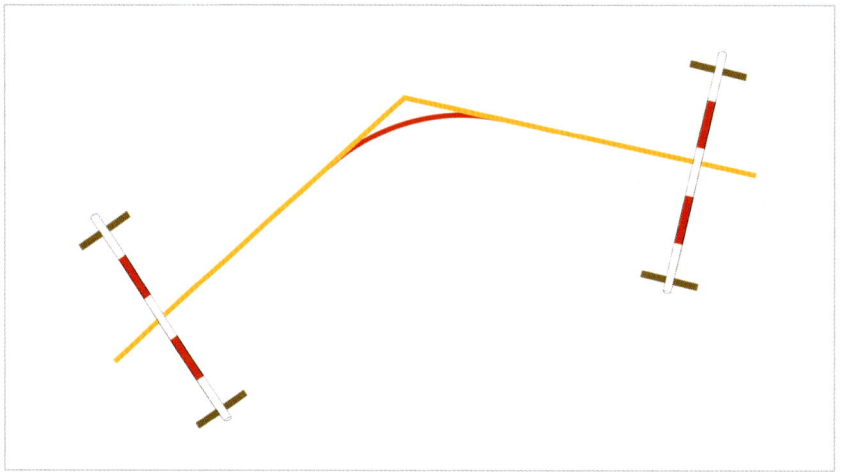

At each jump you should consider what the course designer is asking. What is the test and how does it relate to the next one? Are the jumps related by either distance or technicality? Do not forget the distractions around the arena. The advertising banners, tents, the entrance, and the view beyond the fence can all catch horses unaware if you have not seen them as a possibility for disruption. Do not forget to note where the finish is.

Having walked through the finish, it is important to look away and then repeat the course in detail to a knowledgeable friend without looking back at it to be reminded.

Having walked through the finish, it is important to look away and then repeat the course in detail to a knowledgeable friend without looking back at it to be reminded.

Yes, I did just repeat the sentence twice.

Competition Psychology

My first serious international experience was at an event called Boekelo in The Netherlands. I was raw and enthusiastic, but when I got there and took my horse out for the first time, I looked around and found my confidence seriously jolted. Everyone looked so good, and I began to doubt myself. Without my wife Sue there, giving me support, stability, and belief, it would have been a very difficult few days.

By the end of the weekend, out of the 90 competitors, I finished in the top ten. On the long drive home I had time to reflect on my feelings and emotions. The more I thought about it, the more I came to realize that there were three groups of people at that competition.

1 Those who were happy to be there.

2 Those who were there to complete.

3 Those who were there to compete.

I thought harder and came to the conclusion that there are *always* these three groups of people. At every competition I have ever done, these three groups have been in evidence—from the smallest young-horse schooling show to the Olympic Games as a competitor and a coach. I believe riders consciously or subconsciously decide which group they belong in before arriving at a competition, and as the day progresses, their expectations will be realized. This process happens time and time again—the group that riders feel they belong in will normally determine where they end up: top, middle, or bottom. The top competitors know this, so when they start they already have a good idea of the likely outcome.

The lesser "participants"—for they are not "competitors"—will fulfill their expectations and find reasons to justify why their day went as it did: why they didn't expect any better or why it turned out better than they thought. This may sound harsh, but it is true. Listen to any sports person being interviewed before or after competition. Read into what the competitor says, how it is said, and study the body language.

The same applies to a rider's mindset. Your expectations in training and the standard you decide you want to achieve will translate into your performance at a competition. This mindset can be genetic—some people are born leaders and achievers, while some are happy to be at the other end of the scale—but it can also be possible to alter the outcome with thought of how and a method of application. Where you put yourself defines who you are and where you want to go in the future.

I expect that if you could ask the horse, he, too, will say he belongs in a particular category. History is full of great equine competitors, horses that find a way to win no matter what odds are stacked against them—Valegro in dressage, Big Star in show jumping, and La Biosthetique Sam in eventing—when the rest are there merely to complete.

Prepare to Succeed

It is easy to find great sporting clichés: "You can be great if you want to be," "Dream the dream," "On top of the world." But reality isn't always like

Natural-Born Winners

Head-to-head races favor fast starters, and the legendary racehorse War Admiral's speed from the gate was well known. His old adversary Seabiscuit, on the other hand, was a "pace stalker," skilled at holding with the pack before pulling ahead with late acceleration. In their infamous 1938 match race and its scheduled walk-up start, few gave Seabiscuit a chance to lead War Admiral into the first turn. But Seabiscuit's jockey knew these things and had trained Seabiscuit to run against his type, using a starting bell and a whip to give the horse a Pavlovian burst of speed from the start.

When the bell rang, Seabiscuit broke in front, led by over a length after 20 seconds, and soon crossed over to the rail position. Halfway down the backstretch, War Admiral started to cut into the lead, gradually pulling level with Seabiscuit, then slightly ahead. Following advice he had received, Seabiscuit's jockey eased up, allowing his horse to see his rival, then asked for more effort. A couple hundred yards from the wire, Seabiscuit pulled away again and extended his lead over the closing stretch, finally winning by four lengths, despite War Admiral's running his best time for the distance.

History is full of great rivalries and horses that are *winners*.

that. Opportunities must present themselves, be identified and grasped. So much depends on the individual and your environment: what you have become and what it is possible to become.

An opportunity can come from anywhere: a parent, a coach, a friend, or even a horse. In my case it was twofold. First, it was a bad horse that I swapped for a good one. The good one was a cheap "castoff"—all I could afford at the time—but he eventually turned into a brilliant partner. I always had the mindset that I needed to make the best of what I was presented with. That came from my parents. Secondly, during my time in Ireland as a competition rider I came across a man called Liam Moggan. He was a sports psychologist at the University of Limerick and a remarkable scholar who left an indelible impression on me. He had an unswerving belief in positivity. Everything would have a plus side; good was always there if you looked hard enough. I always came away from our encounters a happier and more positive person. But Liam was also a realist. He knew what could be achieved and how it could be planned. He knew nothing about horses, but he knew people's minds. In applying what I knew, learned, and now want to pass on, I have discovered a number of qualities that become part of the competition rider and the team around them that allows you to compete to the best of your ability. It is called "The Ethics Pyramid."

> Your expectations in training and the standard you decide you want to achieve will translate into your performance at a competition.

Is It Right?

The Growth Mindset　　　**Professionalism**

Relationships　　　**Integrity**　　　**Independence**

What does it mean? Beginning at the base and working up:

Relationships: working together, having a respect for individuals and fellow team members.

Integrity: honesty and strong moral uprightness.

Independence: freedom from the control, influence of others.
These three things provide for a good base for any horseman, especially in competition.

The Growth Mindset: the attitude that things can get better, there is a bigger picture, and thinking outside the box.

Professionalism: an attitude, not a profession, of doing the very best you can.
These are solid qualities to build on top of the base.

Is It Right? It is especially important as an athlete to have a moral compass of right—and more so because you are custodian of the horse.
This, at the top of the pyramid, guides you.

Knowing that you have prepared for a competition with these underlying principles in mind makes you confident that you can withstand the pressures that come your way. These pressures come in all sorts of different guises. It

Keep it Simple

I once took a course walk with an international show jumper, hoping to gain a better insight into how I could improve my skills. We reached Fence 6, and he had said nothing. "So what should I be thinking about up to now?" I asked.

The answer came, "Follow the !@#$%&* numbers!"

There is merit in this simplistic approach, which is often taken by the super-talented athlete. It is certainly uncomplicated and allows the mind to focus only on what is important—jumping the jumps. It is, however, not always possible and needs to be balanced with the equally simple, but more realistic approach which says, "In competition, do what you do well and have practiced at home."

is important that you understand how they appear and what effect they might have on you, and that you also know how they come about and how to deal with them.

Rider Preparation

On the day of the competition it is time to put your plan and teamwork into action. Arriving at the venue with enough time to do all that needs to be done is a priority. If you have a team of helpers, everyone should know who is doing what and how to get it done.

Everyone needs to be able to go to a competition free of any baggage, such as pressures from your daily life—the sorts of things that can play on your mind on the day. Ticking these off will ensure a clear head. Here is a checklist:

- ➤ No undone chores.
- ➤ No shopping to be done.
- ➤ No conversations left half-finished.
- ➤ No people who can't be trusted doing things.
- ➤ No doubts about horse transportation to the competition.
- ➤ No tack in need of a repair.
- ➤ No loose horse shoes.

Coach and Team

It is your coach's job to protect you and your horse from outside issues that appear on the day of competition that you don't need to know about. (Remember that when I say "your coach" it does not necessarily mean the person

Delivery on the Day

Michael Johnson, the American four-time Olympic medalist and BBC Athletics analyst, once said about Mo Farah, Britain's most successful long-distance runner: "Everyone works hard, but it is also about working smart, finding the things that will really make those marginal gains, assessing and diagnosing what areas can improve. What else makes Mo special is his race intelligence and ability to show up on the day and deliver the performance he is capable of. He has done that time and time again."

that helps or teaches you. It could be a parent, a friend, a partner, or anyone involved in your competition effort.) Riders will apply certain pressures—some intentionally, some not—but the coach needs to know how to deal with these, normally by clarifying the aim of the day with you, something that will have been discussed between you before the day. You need to know the "I" in the **team**: What part do "I" (the rider) have in my "team" effort?

Some riders like to be busy, others do not; some like noise, others do not. Moods and feelings can fluctuate during the day for lots of reasons, but these need to be identified and dealt with. The groom looking after the horse will often be one of the first people to get an inkling of a rider's mood and he or she can be a good person to deal with it. I was lucky that my team was always calm on the outside—or maybe I created it.

> **Be realistic about your goals without taking away what might be possible.**

As the competition grows in importance, so the pressure increases. The pressures tend to be the same, they are just increased and so greater attention needs to paid to where they have come from, why they are there, and what to do about them.

One of the tricky things for the coach and the team is being realistic about the goals without taking away what might be possible. When I train riders and their work at home is good enough for a "6 "or "7" out of "10," why should I expect more than this in competition? We must acknowledge that "8s" and "9s" are unlikely. Instead, if they can reproduce the work they do at home in a solid way every time they go out, I have a way of gauging where an expectation might be. Then, realistic goals can be set and achieved.

As a coach I must be careful not to set the bar to an unrealistic height. I have seen this so often and it only produces disappointment for all concerned. Equally, if a pair is doing high quality work at home, then to reproduce it in competition is a fair expectation and should lead to a better end result.

Honest and realistic feedback produces possibilities (see "The Ethics Pyramid," p. 171); hollow praise from the coach or the team is to be avoided.

Final Thoughts

The concept of *Marginal Gains* was first coined by British Cycling at the London Olympic Games in 2012 where the team seemed invincible and won a record number of 12 medals, twice as many as any other team. Much was written about how their manager, Sir David Brailsford, applied this principle. He gambled that if the team broke down "everything" they could think of that goes into competing on a bike, and then improved each element by 1 percent, it would achieve a significant aggregated increase in performance. They reassembled everything with these improvements, and the outcome was remarkable.

I would argue that you can do the same in equestrian sport. If you break down everything into its simplest form and then ask how you can improve it by 1 percent before rebuilding it, your performance can only improve. Plan every transition a little better, improve the quality of the canter to a fence just a little bit, and make every cross-country turn just a little bit tighter to save a vital half-second.

I have heard it said: "If you have five hours to cut down a tree, spend three hours sharpening the axe."

How many of us have been guilty of rushing into a job and hitting it as hard as we can, rather than spending time on doing some preparation?

One of my favorite ideas, however, comes from a philosopher at the University of Calgary called Piers Steel. He says: "Unless you are in a profession where there can only be one winner, like going for Olympic gold, this is pretty good news. With hard work, at the bare minimum you can be good at what you do. And though you might never be the best, you can give the best performers a run for their money.

"On the other hand, if you have chosen a career where only the very, very best succeed, you'd better be born with a lot of talent.

"Necessarily, people who are exceptionally talented are also exceptionally rare. But from what we know, people who work hard are pretty rare too. Most of the time, you are going to end up competing against rivals with one of these attributes, talent, or hard work, not both. Those with natural aptitude and the willingness to put in the effort are as rare as diamonds, and twice as valuable. If you see one, take a picture, get an autograph, and wish him or her good luck....

"Is it better to be hardworking with modest talents or smart but lazy? The answer is cut and dried: hard work wins out. But if you are ready to work hard, to change procrastination into motivation, you now know where to get started."

These words resonate with who I am. I believe that in my sporting career I have exceeded my abilities through dogged determination and hard work. I have identified areas that I can improve and worked hard to make these count. I have appreciated things that I'm not able to improve and diminished their importance. I had a belief that on a good day I can mix it with the best. I also feel lucky that I am able to impart what I have learned, and as a coach give others a way to achieve their potential.

Acknowledgments

Until you start thinking and planning, let alone writing, a book, you have no idea just how many people are actually involved. My time training in the United States has made me many friends and connections. I visit some wonderful parts of the country and am welcomed by a host of great people. Many have given of their time and facilities willingly to allow me to fulfill the aim of getting this into print.

Thank you also to:

My riders.

The wonderful photographers, who followed every move.

Emily, who put life to my diagrams.

To Erin Gallagher and my granddaughter, Hebe who both enlightened me with today's educational theory.

Diagrams by:
Emily Secrett-Hill

Photography by:
Orla Murphy LaScola
Fiona Scott-Maxwell

Irina Kuzmina
Maria Sage
Michele Flanders
Michel Chretinat
Tyree of Smugmug!

Riders:
Meghan Perry
Kelsey Horn
Madison Flanders
Meaghan Marinovich
Sarah Ballou
Izzy Taylor
Sian Hawkes

Locations:
The Vista Schooling and Event Center, Aiken, South Carolina
Inavale Farm, Philomath, Oregon

Finally, I cannot thank Ellie Hughes enough for all her tireless work in bringing order to my thoughts, in being the devil's advocate and a truly wise counsel. I have found working with her a real pleasure and one that I would happily repeat. (She might not agree!)

Index